THE
MYTH & MAGIC
OF
EMBROIDERY

HELEN
STEVENS

THE
MYTH & MAGIC
OF
EMBROIDERY

HELEN M. STEVENS

David and Charles

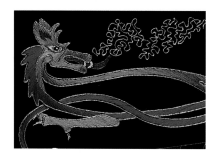

◁ *PLATE 1*
Magic is a personal concept. Embroidery is
a magical medium. Capture what is
magical to you in this spellbinding art.
Here, a miscellany of motifs and ideas blend
together to create a gateway into the fables
and folklore of the countryside. The black
cat beckons you in . . .
19.75 x 29.5cm (7³/₄ x 11¹/₂in)

Helen M. Stevens
Lectures, masterclasses and themed
holidays are available based around
Helen's work. For full details of these
and other products and activities,
including masterclass lessons online,
visit: www.helenmstevens.co.uk

Alternatively, contact Helen via David
& Charles, Brunel House, Forde Close,
Newton Abbot, Devon, TQ12 4PU, UK

For everyone who has
glimpsed the Perilous Realm

A DAVID & CHARLES BOOK
David & Charles is a subsidiary of F+W (UK) Ltd.,
an F+W Publications Inc. company

First published in the UK in 1999
First paperback edition 2005

Text and designs Copyright Helen M. Stevens 1999, 2005
Photography and layout Copyright David & Charles 1999, 2005

Distributed in North America
by F+W Publications, Inc.
4700 East Galbraith Road
Cincinnati, OH 45236
1-800-289-0963

Helen M. Stevens has asserted her right to be identified as author of this work
in accordance with the Copyright, Designs and Patents Act, 1988.

A catalogue record for this book is available from the British Library.

ISBN 0 7153 0774 6 hardback
ISBN 0 7153 2146 3 paperback

Photography by Nigel Salmon, Bury St Edmunds, Suffolk
Book design by Margaret Foster
Printed in China by RR Donnelley
for David & Charles
Brunel House   Newton Abbot   Devon

Visit our website at www.davidandcharles.co.uk

David & Charles books are available from all good bookshops; alternatively you can contact our
Orderline on (0)1626 334555 or write to us at FREEPOST EX2 110, David & Charles Direct,
Newton Abbot, TQ12 4ZZ (no stamp required UK mainland).

CONTENTS

PREFACE

 ONCE again the Story-teller held us in his thrall as he wove his wondrous tales. When last he had been amongst us, the golden sunlight of a warm summer evening had illuminated my Lady's embroidery; now she worked by the steady light of a well-trimmed candle, as the huge fire leaped in the grate and cast dancing shadows against the thick tapestries which lined the walls of the Great Hall. Outside, an icy wind beat against the sturdy timbers and the snow lay thick. My Lord insisted that the Story-teller would not be leaving us this night.

'... *now the young hero, Ragnar, travelled the seas and visited many coasts until he came to the Hall of King Heroth, whose unhappy land was terrorized by two great venomous worms, fire-spitting dragons which daily devoured an ox each and as many men as they could catch. King Heroth had a fair daughter, Thora, whom Ragnar loved, and who came to love him in return, but the King had decreed that no marriage should take place in the land until the worms were slain. Many men had tried, but all had failed, and the damsels of those coasts mourned that their wedding nights seemed destined never to be.*

'*Ragnar was famed for many deeds of valour, but he was only mortal; Thora knew that*

PLATE 3 △

'*O*' *Illuminated initials – letters elaborately decorated to create an eye-catching introduction to the first line of a manuscript – were at their most beautiful and elaborate between the fifth and thirteenth centuries. Whilst this time-span of almost 1000 years is vast, it roughly corresponds to the era of handwritten books in Europe, before the advent of printing which was ultimately to bring about mass production and the inevitable decline in excellence. Throughout this period certain parallels can be drawn between the art of manuscript work and embroidery – hardly surprising, as both were rooted in the Church. Here, a wild boar, symbol of bravery and heroism, leaps forward to begin our tale...*
7.5 x 12.25cm (3 x 4³⁄₄in)

fire and venom would be as deadly to him as to any man, but together they fashioned a strange plan. Thora's ladies wove a great length of woollen fabric, which was cast about his body. The King laughed, "A long cloak will not protect you from the fiery breath of the serpents!"

'The next day, Thora cut and stitched the stuff until she had formed a snug mantle and a pair of breeches which covered Ragnar from head to foot. Again Heroth mocked them. "A close fit will not keep the beasts from stabbing you with their poisonous fangs," he roared.

'That night was as cold and bitter as this. The ice was thick on the river, but Ragnar and Thora broke it and dipped the clothes into the water. Then they lay them out in the starlight. In the morning a fragile white embroidery, the work of the ice maidens, had been worked between every strand of the wool; it glittered like a delicate silver thread, but the mantle and breeches were as hard as iron.

'When Ragnar strode out to meet the great worms their fire was quenched by the water which ran from the strands of ice, but the armour was still strong enough to protect him from their flashing teeth. The enraged serpents flew at him again and again, but each time the ice maidens' embroidery kept him safe. Finally he overcame them both – and the first wedding in the land was his and Thora's.'

My Lord loudly applauded the tale, his thanes and their women called out for more. The children were ushered to bed before another could begin. My Lady smiled softly at the Story-teller and their eyes met before she bent her head to her embroidery and began to couch down another fine silver strand…

Adapted from the *Saga of Ragnar Lodbrog*, a traditional Teutonic legend

◁ *PLATE 2*
The first few flakes to fall herald the magic of a late snow flurry. The seasons hover hesitantly between winter and spring, as the last of the holly berries rival the early aconites (Eranthis hyemalis) in their brilliance. Working on a black background, even a very few snowflakes create a startling effect; fine silver thread, together with white silk, forming tiny filigree discs which immediately draw the eye to the suggestion of movement. Other methods of working snowflakes and raindrops are discussed in later chapters
14.5 x 20.5cm (5³⁄₄ x 8in)

INTRODUCTION

The silken tassel of my purse tear;
And its treasures on the garden throw

The Rubaiyat of Omar Khayyam
Eleventh to Twelfth Centuries

These pearls of thought in Persian gulfs were bred,
Each softly lucent as a rounded moon;
The diver Omar plucked them from their bed,
Fitzgerald strung them on an English thread

James Russell Lowell (1819-91)

IN the silence which followed the applause, a spider scuttled across the straw-strewn floor of the Great Hall. My Lady laughed:

'*There goes the greatest spinner of them all – once a fair lady called Arachne. She challenged Athene – a goddess of some long-ago tribe – to a contest, for she believed that not even a goddess could better her with loom and needle. She wove and stitched a hanging of surpassing beauty; birds, butterflies and flowers rioted as if in very life!*

'*But when the goddess completed her work, it encompassed the whole of creation – great flowing rivers, tall cloud-topped mountains, and every living thing from the tiniest flying insect to the greatest fish in the sea. There was no argument – Arachne had lost the contest, and Athene turned her into a spider for daring to challenge a queen of the heavens. To this day Arachne weaves on – morning, noon and night!*'

PLATE 5 △

'I' Throughout the book, illuminated initials are used to help set the tone for each chapter. Stylized, they can often be adapted for ecclesiastical uses. Here, a simply couched letter is surrounded by stylized pomegranate plants. At its simplest, this is achieved by taking the basic elements of a naturalistic study, such as Fig 1, and working out a pleasing, diagrammatic formula. These ideas will be fully explored as the chapters progress

7 x 12cm (2³⁄₄ x 4³⁄₄in)

'THOSE THAT DEVISE CUNNING WORK' (Exodus 35:35)

In 1611, under the patronage of King James I, and after five years of work by fifty scholars from Cambridge, Oxford and Westminster, the Authorized Version of the Bible was published by the King's Printers. It was hailed as translated from the 'original tongues' which had been 'diligently compared', and each word was chosen with consummate care. Why, then, is spinning, needlework and embroidery constantly referred to in Exodus as 'cunning' work – the executors of such skills as 'wise-hearted'?

Some 400 years earlier the anonymous author of the mystical poem *Sir Gawain and the Green Knight* described the hangings and embroidered linens of a faerie bower as 'cunning-wrought'. A green silk belt, embroidered by hand, has the power stitched within it to protect the wearer from being killed by 'cunning of hand'.

Still earlier, in the Anglo-Saxon tongue, the word 'cunning' was interchangeable with the word 'craft'. 'Wortcunning' was working craft, or magic, with plants, and cunning women, or those who still, perhaps, revered the Old Gods, were forbidden to sew on certain saints' days. The Church, predominantly a man's world, feared the power of women's skills with needle and thread, which in popular belief were still bound up with the thread of life which held body and soul together. Wise women and midwives carried with them a twisted thread to symbolize the mysterious entry into life from the womb, and garments were never mended whilst worn, in case the cutting of the thread brought ill luck, or even death, to the wearer.

In the minds of those fifty scholars, educated men of post-Renaissance England, the idea of embroidery as somehow magic and powerful was too deeply rooted to be questioned. The Ark of the Covenant was covered by a 'vail of blue and purple and scarlet, and fine twined linen' stitched with cherubim, and the robes of the priests embroidered with pomegranates. The breastplate, or tunic, of the high priest was adorned with precious jewels, and it was all *cunning* work (Exodus, Chapters 36 and 39).

In the religion and mythology of almost every known culture there are tales of power and magic inextricably linked with threads, weaving, tapestry and

Fig 1 ▽
More often seen in their stylized form, pomegranates are an attractive motif in both flower and fruit embroidery. Tradition holds that one seed from the thousands in every fruit comes from Paradise – one reason why the pomegranate has always been associated with the Garden of Eden

◁ *PLATE 4 (page 8 – 9)*
A magical image, but one drawn entirely from life. The apple trees on my village green were in blossom one evening, their pastel pink-and-white flowers shimmering in the light of a full moon, across whose face a spider's web spun a fine tracery. On returning from a stroll I found that nature had added a further enchantment. Every tree was surrounded by a halo of glow-worms (Lampyris noctiluca). *Although only the females emit a light, the hovering males*

seem to absorb and reflect their glow, and the treetops were a shifting, glimmering mass of white and silver light.
Never miss the opportunity of noting down an unusual scene – a few lines will do (see Fig 2) – but without something to jog the memory it is difficult to recapture such images. The techniques used to create the effect of light on a black background are fully discussed in Chapters Three and Seven
Embroidery shown life-size:
35.75 x 28.5cm (14 x 11¼in)

. . . .

Fig 2 ▷

April snowflakes can flutter down unexpectedly during the warmest spring. Unwelcome to the fruit grower, they nevertheless suggest a magic combination of effects in embroidery

embroidery. Through centuries of re-telling and translation it becomes difficult to identify with certainty which description applies to particular textile disciplines, but it is impossible to escape the implication that the mystical power wielded by a slender needle and thread far exceeds its physical strength.

Where, then, at the beginning of the third millennium, does this leave lovers of today's embroidery? With more choice than ever before of thread, fabric, and specialist materials of all kinds we are in a unique position. With over 2000 years of tradition behind us, and unparalleled access to research, designs and inspiration at our fingertips through the written word, artwork, photography and now the wonders of cyberspace, we have the opportunity to take embroidery to new heights. The 'new age' has opened the door to elements of interpretative thought which have been lost for generations, and it is no longer considered bizarre to revere nature as more than an infinite resource for the exploitation of humankind. Magic is all around us, in the bursting buds of spring and the fluttering fall of snowflakes, and we ignore it at our peril. The ancient art of embroidery still presents itself as one of the most evocative, appropriate and challenging media in which to capture it.

In my last book, *The Timeless Art of Embroidery*, I explored the history of embroidery as it was recorded and influenced by the last 1200 years. Writing the book was like travelling along a great highway, a journey which witnessed both the momentous events of history and its more intimate moments. Along the way there were many by-roads and detours which invited the traveller to turn aside, but the temptation had to be resisted. No longer – in this book no leafy lane or overgrown track need be ignored, for this is an excursion into the otherworld, away at times from the safety of middle-earth and into the realms of the imagination.

Although few of us may be fortunate enough to actually see a dragon or witness the rites of the fairies, most of us have our own concept of how they might appear. To some a unicorn might be a magnificent animal of mighty proportions, hugely muscled and equipped to overcome all evil by the shattering force of its single horn. To others it might be an elegant, ethereal beast, glimpsed in the mists of dawn, shy and aloof. But whichever interpretation is favoured the depiction of even an imagined realism means adhering to certain rules. The play of light and shadow, use of perspective in foreground and background, and attention to many other such details ensures that your vision of the subject is conveyed with all the vigour and conviction that it deserves. An ongoing study and observation of the natural world will gain us a more satisfactory entry into the realms of the imagination.

Sometimes an actual scene can trigger a quantum leap of inspiration to something more fantastic, as was the case with Plates 8 and 9, but there can be no short cuts between the initial thought, careful observation, meticulous design and preparation before embroidery can begin. Carrying a notebook, jotter, pencil and

◁ *PLATE 6*
In The Timeless Art of Embroidery *passion flowers* (Passiflora caerulea) *were explored as design motifs popular during the Elizabethan era. It was impossible to ignore their mystic parallels with the Passion of Our Lord as interpreted by the Jesuits who first encountered them on arrival in the New World, and it was partly their story which inspired me to delve further into the traditional tales behind other motifs. Many familiar plants have just as fascinating associations, and may be seen in a new light when the background of their folklore is fully understood. Add this to the magic of an imaginative interpretation and your embroidery takes on a whole new dimension*
10.25 x 10.25cm (4 x 4in)

Fig 3 (above left) △
*A 'shorthand' sketch in your notebook, with
arrows to suggest the flow of the design, can be
enough to jog the memory at a later date*

Fig 4 (above right) △
*...back at the drawing board, the scribble in
Fig 3 can be fleshed out and given detail ready
for transfer onto your fabric (see Appendix B)*

coloured crayons to record ideas from nature should have become a habit, so that
when you spot a delightful interlace of stems and stalks, dandelion down and
cobwebs you can note it quickly and simply in your own personal shorthand – a few
pencil lines and a scribble of colour should be enough, with perhaps a few words as
an *aide memoire* to remind you of the more tricky elements (see Fig 3). Back at the
drawing board, perusal of good reference books will enable you to fill in any missing
details. If you are confident that the naturalistic elements of your design are to scale
and correctly coloured, the arrival of a visitor from the 'perilous realm' can be
welcomed as a new challenge (see Chapter One).

   The long and illustrious tradition of embroidery in an ecclesiastic setting has
its origins firmly rooted in the bedrock of history (see *The Timeless Art of Embroidery*).
The early pagan fascination and reverence for the concept of 'thread', spun,
measured and cut by the Fates to determine the pattern and length of life, was
absorbed into Christian iconography, just as early shrines and groves became the
sites of chapels and churches. During the Anglo-Saxon period such embroidery
enjoyed its heyday in the era of *Opus Anglicanum*, declining after the Black Death,
but still an important part of church life, as it remains today. The time-honoured
emblems of the Passion, the Evangelists, the Eucharist and other traditional symbols
have been interpreted variously throughout the ages. I have often been asked
whether my designs could be adapted for such use and the answer is: yes.

   On a practical level, it is important to bear in mind that church embroideries
must be robust enough to survive regular handling; they will rarely be behind glass.

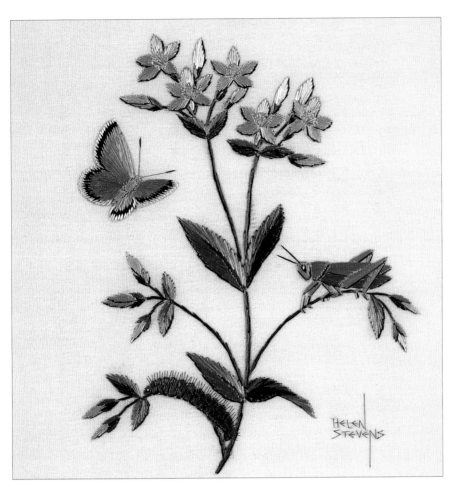

◁ *PLATE 7*
'He made their glowing colours, He made
their tiny wings…' Magic is all around
us in the minutiae of nature. There is no reason
at all why such a study as this could not be
used as a unusual choice to decorate church
vestments or hangings. Because it is small and
detailed the stitches are held firmly to the
background fabric and the basic design could be
used as a 'repeat' to cover a broad area,
such as the central panel of an altar frontal (see
Fig 5). Shown here with common centaury
(Centaurium erythraea) *are the holly blue*
butterfly (Celastrina argiolus), *common field*
grasshopper (Chorthippus brunneus)
and the caterpillar of the white ermine
moth (Spilosoma lubricipeda), *a fine moth*
featured in Chapter One
9.5 x 10.25cm (3³/₄ x 4in)

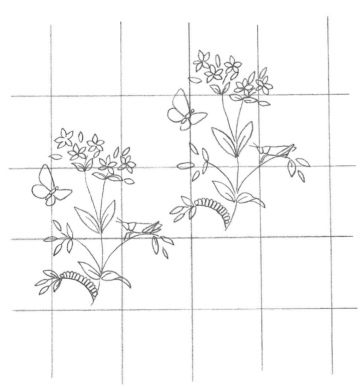

◁ *Fig 5*
A simplified version of Plate 7 can be gridded
onto squared paper to form an overall
repeat pattern. Allow small variations in each
motif to remain, adding to the spontaneity
of the design

· · · · · · · ·

PLATE 8 ▷

*Perhaps because they have a tendency to
spring into life during the hours of darkness,
toadstools and other fungi have the reputation
of existing in both the natural and
supernatural realms. Certainly their names
here read like a spell-binding chant: little
Chinese umbrellas, trooping crumble caps and
the Brownies foot-stool (the infamous fly
agaric, Amanita muscaria). By contrasting
their solid, closely worked shapes with that of
the fly-away head of the dandelion and the
gossamer spider's web the contrast between
light and heavy subjects is emphasized, giving
an extra sense of physical realism to the
embroidery. To complete the scene, the moth
chosen is the ghost swift (Hepialus humuli),
whose habit of hovering over damp meadows
and churchyards gave it its popular folk name*
14 x 16.5cm (5½ x 6½in)

Lectern and pulpit falls will be changed in accordance with the Church's seasons, and altar frontals will be subject to the friction and brushing of passing surplices, amongst other indignities. That said, there is no reason why naturalistic interpretations of nature should not find their place in such locations: the Bible makes many allusions to birds, flowers, and plants which would make suitable subject matter, in addition to the many Christian traditions attached to such motifs.

If realistic studies are not suitable to a given location, either ecclesiastic or secular, stylized iconography may be more appropriate. Just as in miniature work it is necessary to extrapolate the essential qualities of a subject to capture its spirit, so to create stylized works which retain liveliness and character we must become comfortable with certain rules of interpretation, which will be discussed throughout our journey into both familiar and unexpected realms of design.

Gold and silver threads have always been spectacular and rich additions to the palette of colours created by a well-stocked embroidery basket. Alone, they can be fire and ice on a dark background, bringing a spark of life to abstract designs. Together with cottons they enhance texture and provide much needed high and low lights to matt finishes. With pure silk they reach a pinnacle of sumptuous richness, the glow of precious metals subtly contrasting the shimmer of floss and sleave. A natural progression from the use of such threads is towards the addition of semi-precious stones and finely crafted beads.

In creating the collection of embroideries for this book my researches took me along many paths of exploration. To interpret fully the mystical elements of some subjects it became increasingly evident that new dimensions of embroidery, both on practical and abstract levels, would be necessary. In both researching and resourcing semi-precious stones a whole new dimension opened up. Apart from the qualities of colour and texture which they added to both stylized and in some cases naturalistic embroideries, if we are to believe certain new-age theories the very use of such stones imbue our creations with the attributes and properties which they are said to contain. Whether or not we share such beliefs, there can be no doubt that the glow of citrine adds a positive vibrancy to a design, and that the cool, crystalline sheen of amethyst imparts a calming lustre.

Carefully chosen beads can capture the essence of a time and place – such as ancient Egypt – and we should not be afraid to experiment with new specialist threads. Ancient concepts can be expressed in modern materials, just as the modern world has taken to expressing itself in ancient metaphors; the 'worldwide web' of the internet is an exact parallel to the Anglo-Saxon belief that all things in time and space are linked by gossamer threads, embroidering the very fabric of existence. Both are expressed via a web; and in many tribal civilizations the 'triple goddess' is represented by a spider who is, in herself, indistinguishable from the three Fates, determining the dimensions of an individual's existence by the length of a thread.

However we choose to interpret the world about us, it is still a beautiful place, infinitely changing. A sunny afternoon landscape can alter in the space of a few hours to an ethereal moonlit scene of shifting mists and unexpected shadows. To render such subjects faithfully through the medium of embroidery we must begin to

look at entirely new methods of capturing light and shade, of suggesting movement and the translucent properties of mist and starlight. Such scenes, of course, are entirely real, but by opting to study such new areas of design we are already entering into a realm bordering on the supernatural (see Plates 67 and 75, Chapter Seven). Without some understanding of the legends and myths surrounding not only embroidery itself but also the subjects which we choose, a great deal of the joy of such interpretations is lost. Throughout *The Myth and Magic of Embroidery* I have tried to knit together the strands of traditional knowledge, folklore and superstition which are an integral part of the identities of everyday plants, animals and landscapes. Together with the innovative use of both familiar and unusual materials I hope that the images created capture the true magic of the countryside.

'*Eenie, meenie, macca, racca…*' – the opening line of a children's counting game is still to be heard in the playgrounds of rural East Anglia. Incredibly ancient,

Fig 6 ▽
Moonlight can produce strange, stark shadows. Devise a 'shorthand' technique to suggest deep shading without having to sketch in the details. Here, the scribbled tree on the left dominates its smaller companion. In my personal shorthand the symbol above tells me to emphasize the right-hand shadowing of the features

PLATE 9 ▷
Where the Brownies' foot-stool grows, can the fairies be far away? Perhaps a wood fairy has wings like those of the spurge hawk-moth (Hyles euphorbiae), *a visitor to English woodland. Who knows? The wood crane's-bill* (Geranium sylvaticum) *would certainly be an appropriate habitat for both. New techniques such as minuscule speckling (see Chapter One) to create an almost transparent effect are necessary to capture the insubstantial characteristics of a tiny traveller from the otherworld*
12 x 13cm (4³/₄ x 5in)

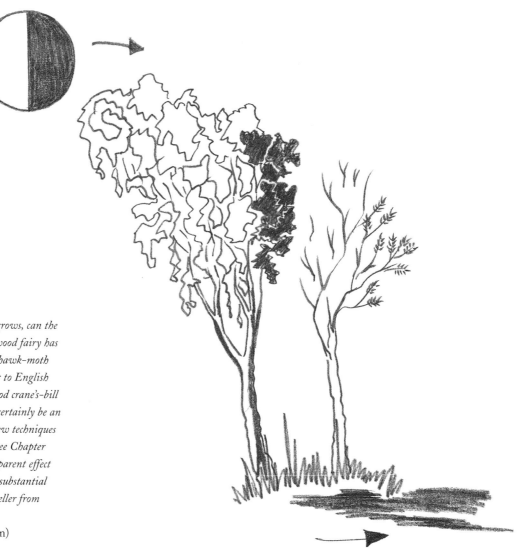

versions of the chant are to be found all over the islands of Britain, their origins in Celtic numerals. English tradition holds that they were used by the 'cunning ones' of the Druids to choose human sacrifices, emissaries to the otherworld, later reborn into their communities. When the Romans conquered much of Britain the Celtic language began its decline, only to be retained by those in solitary occupations such as textile work. The strange Druid chant was still used by needlewomen in the nineteenth century to count their stitches; it seems that the link between needle and thread, life, death and rebirth is still only just below the surface of our own embroideries.

CHAPTER ONE

WORDS AND MUSIC

… Honi soit qui mal y pense, write
In emerald tufts, flowers purple, blue and white;
Like sapphire, pearl, and rich embroidery,
Buckled below fair knighthood's bending knee.
Fairies use flowers for their charactery

The Merry Wives of Windsor
William Shakespeare (1598)

HELEN
STEVENS

OR some time
the Story-teller
remained silent,
watching my Lady as she
stitched, and then he said:

'*Once a fine ealdorman rode out on a clear May morning. Along-side the river he rode, where the lady's slipper and the bryony entwined, and there he espied a maid of faerie-land, slim and slight of form, beckoning him to come to her. Entranced by her strange beauty he jumped the river and caught her round the waist, kissing her three times three. But she was treacherous and slipped from his grasp, calling back to him, "As you came to me of your own free will today, so tonight your life is forfeit and you will come to me again." Aware of his folly, the ealdorman spurred his horse*

homeward until he came to a tall tower, where his own true love fair Eleanor sat, sewing a silver seam. As he began to wish her farewell forever, already feeling a strange malady come upon him, he fell to the ground in a swoon. Fair Eleanor laid him in her bed, and sent her servant maid to fetch a sheet woven and stitched with silver by her own hand to lay over him. When dawn came his strength was restored, the faerie-maid's enchantment was lifted and when he wed fair Eleanor that very day, she wore a gown of shimmering silver.'

PLATE 11 △

'F' *This relatively simple design is given its intricacy by the scrolling couched silver threads. The initial itself is first embroidered in snake stitch, then outlined in gold thread, again surface couched (there is discussion of this technique later in this chapter).*
The flowers used to frame the initial are stylized periwinkles. An evergreen, the lesser periwinkle (Vinca minor) was regarded during the medieval period as a symbol of immortality, in common with many non-deciduous plants, and would make a pretty overall design suitable for church hangings. Each flower has a regular, five-petalled face, with a white eye, and the leaves are symmetrically paired, making it an easy motif to draw, either as a repeat pattern or a random design (see Fig 7).
Keep the scale small so that the radiating stitching in both petals and leaves is not susceptible to damage
8.75 x 12cm (3½ x 4¾in)

THE SILVER SEAM

Folk songs and fairy tales, nursery rhymes and proverbs: all seem to come to our lips unbidden. We are rarely aware of having learned them; they are just there, waiting for the right opportunity to come to the forefront of our minds. So much of our ethnic identity is bound up in these folk memories that we take them for granted. We do not analyze them; they are simply part of the rich pattern which forms our childhood and which, in adult life, becomes a patchwork quilt of snippets and quotes ready for any occasion. Goldilocks, on her fine cushion, sewing a fine seam; the merits of 'a stitch in time'; the mice (in folklore, fairies) who help the Tailor of Gloucester and others; all are as familiar as our own childhood bedrooms, havens of comfort and security.

Little might we imagine that many ancient tales and songs have their origins in the pagan rites of a time before Christianity reached northern Europe, when the 'cunning ones' were in contact with the Old Gods and it seemed natural to expect the otherworld and this to intermingle from time to time. The use of the metaphor of needle and thread, of the ability to mend what is torn, decorate what is plain and bind what is loose, can be traced through aeons of time, from anonymous country songs and dances, through a dalliance with respectability in the shape of the classic poets, to the crude rustic songs of recent centuries and the banal rugby club songs of today.

Fair Eleanor and her silver seam is an embodiment of that part of the 'triple goddess', mother, mistress, murderess who can give birth to, or even resurrect, her offspring, lover, victim by the use of some symbolic and powerful tool – in this case the beauty of her needlework. She appears again as the Lady of Shalott, prisoner in

Fig 7 ▷

A random carpet design can be achieved by roughing out arabesques and coiling tendrils first, and adding flowers, leaves and so on at various intervals along its length

◁ *PLATE 10 (page 20 – 21)*

The way into faerie-land was often to be found in overgrown places beside streams or through the sides of hills – the fine ealdorman should have known better than to trust a fey stranger on the river bank! By tradition 'faerie' is the archaic name for the otherworld (we might call it another dimension today); 'fairies' are only one species of its inhabitants, a diminutive, secretive race. Tall, regal, residents were 'faeries', and these more often beautiful, fascinating but frequently dangerous individuals were known to lure humans into the perilous realm. Elves, too, occasionally crossed the divide to intervene in human matters. As well as the butterflies and ladybirds there is another little winged character hiding in this picture.

Its sprays of greenish-yellow flowers, followed by colourful clusters of berries, give no clue as to why this bryony is called 'black'. In fact, it is an allusion to the tuberous black root, poisonous until boiled, when it becomes edible like other members of the yam family. The whole plant is toxic, and cattle can become addicted to it, sometimes dying as a result; in the Middle Ages they were thought to be 'elf-shot' in this condition and under the sway of supernatural influences. Fine elfin complexions were thought to be attainable by applying the juice of the berries to remove freckles and other skin blemishes.

The small blue (Cupido minimus) *is the tiniest butterfly in Britain, as its Latin name suggests, and was once thought to be a harbinger of romance. When first hatched their wings bear the same iridescent scales as other blue butterflies, but their habitual flight through low ground-cover plants quickly wears these away until the butterflies gradually lose their colour, their wings become ragged and their loss of flight results in their falling prey to predatory birds, an analogy of youth and the sorrows of unrequited love!*

Embroidery shown life-size:
38 x 26.5cm (15 x 10½in)

· · · · · · · ·

the four grey towers overlooking a space of flowers in Tennyson's epic poem, herself the victim of enchantment as 'she weaves by night and day a magic web with colours gay'. A bawdy Suffolk song of the nineteenth century is still more explicit in its association of thread with the giving of life:

> *Oh, it was on a summer's day, in the merry month of May*
> *And all the flowers were in bloom,*
> *I met a pretty miss, and I asked her for a kiss,*
> *And to wind up her little ball of yarn.*

Nine months later, the singer meets the pretty miss, with a baby on her arm, and asks 'Who would ever have thought this, when I wound up your little ball of yarn.'

However diverse the interpretations of Eleanor's story, two elements remain constant: the thread and the flowers which bloom around her. The faerie realm and flowers are inseparable – as Shakespeare notes – and they are a fine starting point for our interpretations of the otherworld. In Plate 10, the lady's slipper orchid (*Cypripedium calceolus*) is entwined by black bryony (*Tamus communis*), two plants which take us back to basics in our methods of embroidery. In a study such as this, apparently simple and yet intricate in construction, a very limited palette of colours has been used – only nine in the floral elements of the design – and so the use of high and low lighting, and a variety of gauges of thread, is important to effect realism.

Black bryony is a climbing plant, though with a rather shambling habit, loosely twining itself around its neighbours without damaging them. In the Middle Ages its toxic properties were well known, and the beautiful yet highly poisonous berries thought to be a valuable addition to witches' more harmful potions. The coiling stems and tendrils should be shadowed in stem stitch, and worked similarly, beginning with a fine gauge of thread at their apexes, gradually thickening towards the more solid branches at the core of the plant. Its broad, heart-shaped leaves are natural candidates for the use of sweeping *opus plumarium* to describe their glossy surfaces. These two techniques, variously adapted, form the basis of much of the embroidery in this book, and a full description of their working, and the execution of other elementary stitches, can be found in Appendix A (page 124). Working the *opus plumarium* towards the core tip of each fruit similarly creates the shiny, wax-like berries.

The lady's slipper was named for 'Our Lady' in Christian times, yet in earlier ages its wearers were thought to be of a very different realm: the inhabitants of Faerie. Uniquely among the orchids of the British Isles, it bears large single blooms, each with a pouting, hollow lower lip – the 'slipper' of its common name. To create a lifelike interpretation of this unusual shape we must analyze minutely the directional stitching, and it is easier to start by examining a much simpler flower, such as the common evening primrose (*Oenothera biennus*), shown in Plate 12.

In colour not dissimilar to the lip of the lady's slipper, the evening primrose allows us to explore the principle of directional *opus plumarium* without the difficulty of too complicated a shape. Remember that stitches must fall backwards towards the

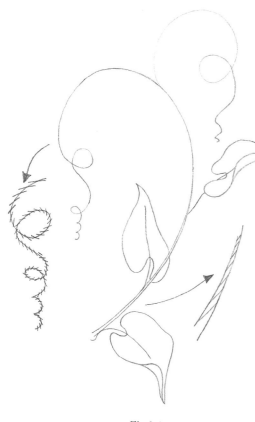

Fig 8 △

Stem stitch may vary in length and thickness according to the shape to be described. It is always easier to begin at the apex of each motif, such as at the tip of the tendril, stem, vein, and so on. A coiling tendril (left) should be worked in fine thread, gradually thickening towards the stem. Begin with short, closely worked stitches, opening out into longer, less overlapping ones as the tendril progresses. On the main stem (right) thicken the motif by using a higher gauge thread and allowing the stitches to overlap more

◁ *PLATE 12*
Often the simplest designs can be the most effective. Both this, and the subject of Plate 13, were scenes glimpsed in my own garden. The evening primrose is a garden plant which has been a successful escapee into the wild and is now often found on waste ground. Its handsome four-petalled, cup-shaped blooms open in succession along a tall spike, mostly surviving for only a night and day, their delicate fragrance attracting a wide variety of insects. The white ermine moths were frequent visitors, and soothed by the apparently soporific effect of the perfume allowed the gentle onlooker to lightly stroke their beautiful, furry bodies. To recreate this furry effect, work the upper bodies of the insects in fine thread, allowing several narrow strata of stitching to radiate from the head downwards. Working on black, allow a fraction of the background fabric to show through the stitches to emphasize the fluffy effect, contrasting this by using four closely embroidered strata, separated by voiding (See Appendix A, page 124) to create the abdomen section
9.5 x 11cm (3³⁄₄ x 4¹⁄₄in)

core of any given motif, no matter how complex that motif may, at first, appear. In a simple, broad-petalled plate-shaped flower, this is easy to follow (see Fig 9). Where necessary allow stitches to disappear behind their neighbours to advance the angle of the flow, and where the petal appears to reflex against itself, follow the rules which apply to opposite angle embroidery (see Appendix A, page 124). Applying these rules to the bulbous pouch of the lady's slipper, shadow line where the lip

◁ *Fig 9*
Left: The open face of the evening primrose is worked in simple radial opus plumarium.
In Plate 12 the lower petal has curved forwards to reveal its underside, in which case opposite angle embroidery would be used.
Compare the two
Right: The bulbous lip of the lady's slipper orchid should be worked in two or more strata, carefully angled to allow the stitches to 'fall back' to the growing point

PLATE 13 ▷

*Bright red, vivid blue, black and white – it is
difficult to believe that such vibrancy can
be a common sight in the mortal realms, but
the morning glory scrambling high in
mid-summer against the dark wood of my barn
was frequently visited by the superb red
admiral* (Vanessa atalanta). *This butterfly's
eighteenth-century name was the 'admirable'
from which its present name derives, but it was
previously called the 'alderman', or 'ealdorman',
a still earlier term for an earl or aristocrat,
as its wings so closely resembled the liveries
of noblemen.*

*In order to ensure that the black-upon-black
stitching of the upper wing is discernible, the
white scallops at the outer edge of the wing
should be carefully emphasized, worked at the
same angle as the main fields of radial work, to
create an effective outline. On the uppermost
edge of the wing, the sweep of the stitches will
catch the light and reflect it, so ensuring that
the contrast of texture between embroidery and
background fabric does a similar job*

9 x 10.25cm (3½ x 4in)

crinkles as it curves backwards and work two strata of *opus plumarium* curving to follow the flow of the overall shape (Fig 9). Infill the hollow centre of the lip in dark grey to create an area of deep shadow. The outer petals, leaves and other elements of the plant may then be worked in simple directional stitching.

We can also use Plate 12 to simplify the dalmatian dog technique (Appendix A, page 126) which has been used on the large Queen of Spain fritillary butterfly (*Argynnis lathonia*) in Plate 10. The wings of the white ermine moths (*Spilosoma lubricipeda*) are perfect examples. Working the black spots first, at an angle which will match the overall sweep of the rest of the wing, embroider the main field of the wings around them, creating a smooth, single plane of stitching. Use exactly the same technique in the more complex design on the wing of the butterfly.

All these techniques may also be practised in a study such as Plate 13. The simplistic format of the evening primrose is taken one step further in the convolvulus, as the stitches 'fall through' the trumpet of the flower into its throat, the core in this case being where the sepals appear at its foot. Dark grey shading again suggests deep shadow. Dalmatian dog technique and the smooth blending of several strata of *opus plumarium* complete the red admiral butterfly.

BUDS, BUTTONS AND BEADS

It is perhaps inevitable that fairies and flowers should be so closely associated, when one comes to consider the limited materials available to fairy dressmakers and tailors! A tiny person requires tiny clothes, and in many descriptions of encounters with the 'little people', those who happen upon them unawares have later gone to great lengths to detail their fashions. We need only suspend our disbelief to enjoy their descriptions.

On new year's morning 1626 the queen's chambermaids espied Oberon, King of the Fairies, and later described him to the poet Simon Steward. '*His belt was made of Mirtle leaves, Pleyted in small curious theaves Besett with Amber Cowslip Studdes, and fringed about with daysie budds.*' Titania, Queen of the Fairies, together with flowers, was said by Shakespeare to wear the 'enamell'd skin' thrown aside by a snake, and in Richard Johnson's *History of Tom Thumbe*, in the early seventeenth century, he writes that Queen Mab, midwife of the fairies, provided Tom with a '*very artificiall sute of apparell*', his '*Band and Shirt being both sowed together, was made of Spider's Cobweb*'. Our embroideries are limited to somewhat less bizarre materials, but nevertheless it is possible to capture something of that ethereal, miniature world.

Plates 12 and 13 have helped with our revision of flatwork embroidery techniques, so we are now ready to approach rather more complicated and delicate subjects. Plate 14 brings us down to the size of a Tom Thumb or Thumbelina, and we find ourselves on a level with harebells and daisies. One of the difficulties in creating lifelike interpretations of wildflowers is in eliminating elements of their habitat which would confuse our designs. Both harebells (*Campanula rotundifolia*) and daisies (*Bellis perennis*) are grassland plants, normally to be found stretching their heads above a tangle of green blades and seeds (see Fig 10). These need to be removed from our sketch to reveal the elegant curves of the harebells' stems and the stocky, rounded leaves of the daisy.

We can then begin to study the form of the flowers themselves, both of which are very different. Working on a pale background, a shadow line is essential, even on the shaded side of each of the tightly packed petals of the daisy, where it will separate them and emphasize their individuality. The common name of the daisy derives from 'day's eye', each flower a tiny sun, surrounded by rays of light in the shape of its petals, which close at night. Densely worked seed stitches (Appendix A, page 127) describe the yellow sun disc at the centre of each flower, and narrow wedges of *opus plumarium* in white, the petals themselves. A blush of pink is achieved by working a shooting stitch (Appendix A, page 126) of pale pink into some of the petals.

The harebells may be approached similarly to the convolvulus in Plate 13, though in a finer gauge of thread. The core of each flower is at the point where the sepals join the bell and the arcs and wedges of *opus plumarium* should fall back to that point. Simple directional stitching for the leaves of the daisy and snake stitch (Appendix A, page 126) complete the sinuous leaves of the harebells. A feeling of movement is provided by the butterfly and bee.

Fig 10 △
The elegant lines of such flowers as harebells and daisies can be confused by including too many surrounding grasses, as shown here. These elements can be removed when the final sketch is made for transfer

PLATE 14 ▷

'Fairy bells', 'witches thimbles' and 'old man's bells' are all folk names for the fragile harebell – the 'old man' in this case being the Devil – so closely were they associated with magic. Their curious nodding habit, which seems to occur even without a discernible breeze, led the credulous to believe that Brownies (Scottish sprites) were pulling invisible bell ropes. The daisy, by contrast, was a flower of the sun, guileless and cheerful. Geoffrey Chaucer claimed the daisy as his favourite flower, the only one which could 'soften all my sorrow', and featured it in his Legend of Good Women. *In embroidery, as with all arts, there can be no substitute for personal observation, the closer the better. Only by getting down to the level of your subjects can you really appreciate their form and interaction (see Fig 10) – and it is a marvellous excuse for lying full-length in the warm sunshine!*
8.25 x 11cm (3¼ x 4¼in)

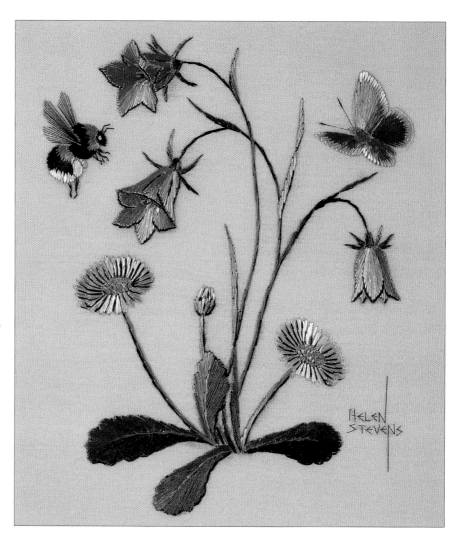

The tiny size of the daisy bud can be estimated by comparison to the bumble bee – no wonder Oberon chose that his belt should be set about with buttons in the shape of daisy buds; their pleasing rounded shape suggests to even the most sceptical that a fairy could make good use of them. The buds of the cowslip, his 'studdes', would be slightly more pointed, and similar in shape to those of the water violet, the only aquatic member of the primrose family (Plate 15).

Some fairies, of course, need no clothes. On a balmy summer morning the water is warm, the water violets provide shelter and dewdrops on a gossamer cobweb give a little camouflage to the shy, honeycomb-winged, river fairy. To create the translucent effect the fairy's body needs a completely new technique. Look at it closely and it seems almost to disappear before your eyes – there is, in fact, no corporeal edge, no directional work and no regimented, abutting stitches. The flesh is made up of minuscule speckling stitches, each covering no more than one strand of the fabric, which is a fine, but dense, evenweave cotton.

Sketch and transfer your little character just as you would a tangible subject (see Appendix B, page 133). Work the details of the face in a very fine gauge of thread, emphasizing the eyes with eyelashes and highlights. Using no more than three colours, light and dark flesh tones and grey, work the whole area of the skin in speckling. When this is complete, suggest an outline to the lower edges of the figure, and to separate the limbs, by overlaying straight stitches in black. The finished effect will be matt and incredibly fine. Work the hair in fine zigzags of gold-coloured and fine black silk, speckling randomly along the waves with a fine blending filament. The wings are worked similarly to a dragonfly's (see page 127), given an opalescent sheen by overlaying the cellophane film separated from a blending filament.

A gossamer canopy stretches from the tip of the water-violet buds to the lily pad, overlaying the embroidery beneath. To create the illusion of droplets of water slipping down the strands, whip tiny ice-blue seed beads onto your thread and allow the weight of the beads to describe a concave curve. Take a stroll in the garden at dawn when the cobwebs are spangled with dew: the effect is identical.

We do not have to enter the realms of complete fantasy to witness creatures just as ethereal and delicate as the river fairy. Common bindweed is the foodstuff of the fragile white plume moth (*Pterophorus pentadactylus*), its pure white wings forming five feathery plumes on either side of its papery body (Plate 16). At rest,

◁ *PLATE 15*
Featherfoil is perhaps the more appropriate folk name for the water violet (Hottonia palustris), which is no relation to the violet family. The feathery leaves of the plant usually remain underwater, except in warm weather when the water level falls and their delicate green whorls become visible. The tall, filigree qualities of this plant prove a perfect contrast in terms of design with the dense flat plate of the lily-pad, with its bullet-shaped bud and round-bodied flower. The yellow water-lily will be explored in greater depth in Plate 28.
The addition of the tiny seed beads to this picture add a sense of the three-dimensional. Not only does the supporting thread overlay background features, but the beads themselves cast an actual (rather than an embroidered) shadow which adds to the illusion. The mayfly is worked simply in a straight winged technique (Appendix A, page 127) to avoid clashing with the complex structure of the river fairy's dragonfly wings
12.25 x 12.25cm (4³/₄ x 4³/₄in)

PLATE 16 ▷

The combination of scrolling arabesques in both silk and metallic thread give added interest to this simple study. By limiting the use of the gold thread to the tendrils a certain restraint is effected, which allows the use of specialist threads in a naturalistic setting, without leaning too far towards stylization. This design choice has also been used in Plate 13

10.25 x 10.25cm (4 x 4in)

Fig 11 △

The ethereal white plume moth can be easily achieved using the correct order of working. From the top: Work the body in small lozenges of satin stitch, followed by the central veins of the feather-like wings. Working the upper edge of each vein first, in short straight stitches at 45 degrees to the vein, complete each wing, beginning at the top. Bottom: At rest the moth adopts a characteristic 'T' shape

bottom left, the lower wings are drawn up under the upper, giving it a characteristic 'T' shape, whilst in flight it has an erratic, fluttering habit. Most effective worked on a black background, by superimposing at least part of a wing over another feature, such as the bindweed stem, centre right, the diaphanous quality of the plumes becomes most apparent. Work each plume separately, the central vein first, in fine stem stitch, radiating short straight stitches, at a 45 degree angle, along its length. By working along the upper edge of the central vein first in each case, the convex curve of each plume will be pulled into place. A single long straight stitch in fine silver thread creates each antenna (see order of working in Fig 11).

The pretty pink-and-white flowers of the bindweed exude a sweet almond-scented odour which attracts many insects, although they rarely pollinate successfully and spread by means of an extensive and extremely tenacious root system. The young shoots of the bindweed can force themselves up through rock-hard topsoil, and right through tarmac and other man-made surfaces. If not actually witnessed, it is hard to believe that such a delicate plant, with its finely coiling tendrils, can deserve one of its many folk names – devil's guts. A touch of metallic gold thread, held down by a gold-green silk to create the twisting curlicues of its coils, introduces us to a technique which can be stylized or naturalistic depending upon its application – surface couching.

THE ALCHEMIST'S STONE

When Christian missionaries first began to preach in England they received a mixed welcome. To some the 'new' God was simply another to add to the pantheon they already worshipped; to others He was an enemy to be resisted implacably, but gradually the new religion began to take the ascendant. Many shrines and groves dedicated to earlier deities were realigned to form chapels and churches, many traditions and festivals similarly absorbed, as the midwinter solstice fused with Christmas, spring rites with Easter and autumn festivals of the dead with All Hallows' Day. The Romano-Celtic peoples had also suffered tangible invasions, first from the Saxons, whose intermarriages gave rise to the Anglo-Saxon civilization, and who in turn were attacked, even more destructively, by the Vikings and Danes. But successive assimilations took place, and by the tenth century Celtic Christianity thrived side-by-side with influences from Saxon and Viking, its own ethos more threatened by the rulings of Rome.

High stone crosses still survive in places, often fragmented, but remaining powerful images attesting to the beliefs of their sculptors. Plate 17 is inspired by a stone sculpture on the tenth-century cross shaft at St Alkmund's church in Derby. Rarely is a marriage of Anglo-Saxon and Scandinavian influences so apparent as in this design of a full-bodied zoomorphic animal, loosely entwined in a ribbon

◁ PLATE 17
There are many different types of gold thread on the market, ranging from the very fine, single strand which can be threaded on a fine needle, several stranded threads which can be used in their original format or split down, through to heavy gauges suitable only for couching purposes. Within that range they may be smooth, Jap, passing, and so on. The choice of thread must be made bearing in mind the use to which they will be put. Here, a bright Jap gold has been chosen as it readily fills the broad fields to be covered. An archaic effect is achieved by spiralling the thread within each field, ignoring the contours of the ribbon interlace, whilst a more contemporary effect is created by working the couching in a linear pattern, following the course of the ribbonwork, such as has been used in the initials 'O' and 'T' in Plates 3 and 5
(see also Fig 13)
6.5 x 7.5cm (2½ x 3in)

interlace formed of its own tongue. It is framed in a smoothly rounded arcade – so much for the stonemason's input. Surmounting a robust jigsaw of colours, a simplified version of Anglo-Saxon embroidery design, it could work well today as the central panel of a lectern or pulpit fall. It is an ideal piece with which to begin an exploration of couched work and split stitch which we can later elaborate into more complex designs, suitable for ecclesiastic or secular purposes.

Surface couching is an age-old technique for securing gold or other precious thread to the background fabric without 'wasting' any of such a valuable commodity on the reverse of the material. Split stitch is a similarly thrifty method of effecting complete coverage of a large area of background fabric, again allowing only the minimum amount of thread to be invisible. Not only economical, both techniques are also practical, as the threads are held firmly to the fabric, with little chance of their being snagged, pulled loose, or distorted by external conditions. Transfer your design in the usual way (see Appendix B).

There is no attempt at realism in this type of work, and so outlining is just that – outline every element of the motif in a vibrant colour (red is ideal), using stem stitch where the outline curves and split stitch along straight lines. Split stitch is worked by taking a small straight stitch and bringing the needle up through the stitch, leaving just a small dot of thread on the reverse of the fabric, subsequently taking your second stitch, the same length as the first, along the contour to be effected. By working backwards and forwards, rather than always in the same direction to infill the coloured mosaic forming the background of the design, all that shows on the back of the work is a series of tiny dots. Terminate areas of colour abruptly so that a sharp, clean break is effected.

Only when all the areas of colour have been worked should we begin to apply the gold thread. Plate 17 is worked in Jap gold, the metallic foil wrapped loosely around the core of the thread. Stitches in the couching thread should therefore be worked in such a way that they lie over the foil, not slipping down between the coils. The secret of surface couching is to work the stitches at regular intervals, the distance between them to be estimated by the acuteness of the various contours. Broad open contours allow the couching stitches to be further

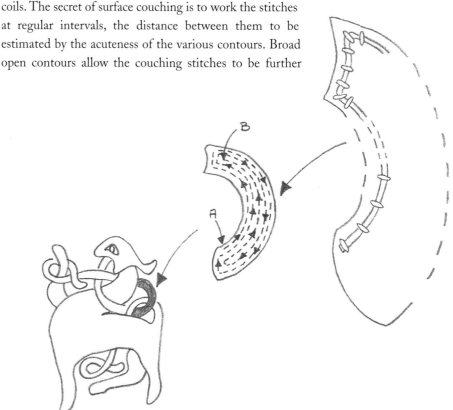

Fig 12 ▷
Each section of the ribbon interlace design
should be fully worked before continuing to the
next. For the reverse 'C' shape shown, begin at
point A, working clockwise in a decreasing
spiral, finishing at point 'B'. Couching stitches
should be closer together where the angle of the
spiral is greatest

apart than would be necessary for sharp, 'hairpin' bends. Whip down the ends of the gold thread at the beginning and end of each section and continue in a spiral pattern until the full field of each section of the motif is filled (see Fig 12).

Plate 18 shows a more complicated design. To the left, the outlined ribbon interlace is shown at the top of the piece, whilst the jigsaw motif of split stitch colours is completed in the arcade beneath. One half of the asymmetric design has been completed in gold, the other left to show the linen below, extrapolating the design. To the right, the reverse of an identical piece shows just how economical the disciplines are – it seems impossible that such a rich, dense piece of work should be so sparsely mirrored. This design will be explored in more depth in Chapter Seven.

In alchemy, the much sought-after 'stone' was believed to have the ability to transform base metal into gold. The ancient stonework of the Anglo-Saxons seems an ideal catalyst for translating rock into a tactile, colourful textile.

◁ *Fig 13*

In this knotwork device the ribbon interlace begins to the right of each motif, and progresses through the design as indicated by the black arrows (left). In the archaic arrangement of the couched threads, each section would be worked in a spiral, independently of the overall design (centre). In a modern interpretation, the 'ribbon' effect can be emphasized by allowing the couched threads a linear passage through the knot (right)

CHAPTER TWO

BLITHE SPIRITS

That certain night, the night we met,
There was magic abroad in the air;
There were angels dining at the Ritz
And a nightingale sang in Berkeley Square

Maschwitz/Sherwin, 1940

HELEN
STEVENS

HER eyes still bent upon her needlework, my Lady spoke as if to herself:

'Yes, embroidery can wield its magic upon many levels, as a giver of life and a bringer of justice. I heard of a tale told by the Romans, from a time long before even their history began, when the evil King of Thrace, Terseus, lusted after his wife's sister Philomela, whose sweet singing aroused his passion. She was noble and chaste, but he dishonoured her, cutting out her tongue so that she could tell no one of her plight. She escaped from his hall, but wished to send word to Queen Procne, her sister, of Terseus' treachery. Afraid that a letter might be intercepted by the king, she embroidered a purple robe with the story, and sent it to her. When the queen read and understood the tale, she fled from the king, arriving at her sister's side with Terseus in pursuit. As he was about to kill them both, the gods intervened, turning Philomela into a nightingale and her sister into a swallow. To this day the sweet-tongued nightingale is called by some the embroiderer's bird.'

PLATE 20 △

'H' *No bird is the subject of more myth and superstition than the magpie (Pica pica), the most familiar being the old chant of 'One for sorrow, two for joy…'. To protect themselves from the misfortune brought about by the sighting of a single magpie, the superstitious would spit three times, raise their hat to the bird or sing 'Devil, Devil, I defy thee'. I prefer the more polite greeting to the single magpie, 'Good morning, your Majesty, and how's her Ladyship?'*
This initial is rather art nouveau, in the style of the William Morris Arts and Crafts movement. The Celtic influence is still apparent in the interlace of the letter itself, the other components being slightly more realistic. The stem of the stylized traveller's joy is worked in the same 2/1T thread as is used in Plate 24, surface couched to create a smooth effect. At its base real, roughly cut amethysts give a three-dimensional lift to the design
9.5 x 12.5cm (3¾ x 5in)

A LITTLE BROWN BIRD SINGING

Often, it seems, the plainest little birds have the finest voices. The nightingale and the skylark have both captured the imagination of poets and writers throughout the ages, from the Classics to the lyrics of some of our favourite songs today. In embroidery it is often tempting to assume that the more colourful the bird, the more attractive it will prove as a subject, but this is not always the case. The subtle golds, browns and beiges of nature's palette translate particularly well into the embroidered medium, where their tones can be varied and enhanced by changes in directional stitching, whether worked on a dark or pale background.

Using the haunting war-time ballad 'A Nightingale Sang in Berkeley Square' as inspiration, the study in Plate 19 (page 34–35) gradually came to life. To capture the feeling of moonlight, silver-greens have been used throughout on the foliage, and silver thread, couched to suggest the tendrils of the sweet peas, links the various shades together. It is important when constructing a large design such as this to have continuity between the subjects; make sure at the drawing-board stage that your various elements bloom, fruit, and so on at the same time of year (in this case mid-May to June).

The song of the nightingale (*Luscinia megarhynchos*) is magic indeed. Plutarch and Aristotle maintained that adult birds taught their offspring the songs and melodies of their forefathers, and that if kept in captivity they would not sing so sweetly; certainly nothing speaks so eloquently of freedom as the nightingale's gentle notes when heard across the open meadows of the countryside. The nightingale is a thrush, closely related to the robin but, unlike its cousin, it is shy and rarely glimpsed; it can be identified by its long chestnut tail, held straight down when perched to sing. This russet tail is the only colourful part of the bird, but in embroidery the rich browns of its upper body and cool beige of its underparts blend together in strata of *opus plumarium* to create a creamy, *café au lait* effect. Following the rules of radial stitching (Appendix A, page 124) begin at the head of the bird, allowing the stitches to fall back evenly. Without radical changes in shade on the upper body it is possible to achieve a particularly smooth effect as head and neck blend with upper back and wing. Repeat the process on the belly.

An open beak should be worked with particular attention to detail and directional stitching (see Fig 14). Seen at a slight angle, a small area of the inside of the mouth is visible and this should be worked in a rich red, similar to the warbling tongue. This suggestion of movement, together with the highlight in the eye, is all that is necessary to bring the bird to life.

⊲ PLATE 19 (page 34 – 35)
The song of the nightingale is the sound of summer. By September the birds have returned to their winter home in Africa. Although they occasionally sing during daylight hours, the melody is often lost amid the chorus of other birds; at night the stage is theirs alone. Similarly the night-scented stock comes into its own after dark. The single flowers are the poor relations of their more spectacular cousins, the double- or treble-bloomed Brompton or ten-week stocks, but that marvellous fragrance is unique, and when the petals unfurl at sunset they are unparalleled.
The emperor moth (Saturnia pavonia) is among the most spectacular of its kind, and is the only member of the silk moth family native to Britain, although its cocoons are not suitable for commercial silk production. Its large 'false eyes' are designed to scare away predatory birds and animals and are excellent motifs on which to perfect dalmatian dog technique, as each succeeding sphere of colour must be built up around is predecessor.
The female, to the left, is larger than the male, and occasionally suns herself during the day, hence the need for the defensive eye markings.
Both the male and female are explored in greater depth in Chapter Five, Plate 55
Embroidery shown life-size:
38 x 28cm (15 x 11in)

Fig 14 ▷
The stitches creating the bird's beak will flow towards its tip – on an open beak this means 'splitting' the motif and working towards twin cores

PLATE 21 (detail of Plate 19) ▷
The female catkins of the London plane tree are
attractive motifs – elegantly drooping,
pendulous pompons of green and crimson.
To master details such as this it is important to
have a wide range of gauges in various
threads so that a convincing contrast is created
between the broad stem of the fruit, worked
in a three-stranded, loose green silk (3/1F) and
a single fine thread of red. There is a full
discussion of how to vary your collection of
thread sizes by twisting your own mixes in
Appendix B. For the stitching techniques used
in this detail, see Fig 15
Detail shown: 10 x 10cm (4 x 4in)

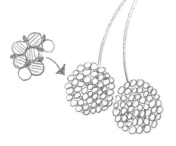

Fig 15 △
Male and female catkins of the London
plane tree
Top: The male catkin is a series of small
spheres, worked simply in tiny areas of satin
stitch, each angled slightly differently, and
interspersed with seed stitches
Bottom: The female catkin is initially worked
similarly to the male, then overlaid with tiny
sunbursts of fine red silk. These are created by
little rosettes of straight stitches, allowed to
overlap at their extremities

The London plane tree (*Platanus x acerifolia*), acting as a perch for our songbird, is a particularly attractive motif. The young leaves are thickly pubescent and velvety to the touch, an effect emphasized by using two shades of silvery gold together in a single needle on the underside of each leaf. This creates an illusion of more than one texture and suggests their slightly immature qualities. Apart from working certain areas in this bi-shaded 2/1F thread (see Appendix B, page 132) they are simply stitched in single fields of radial embroidery – one strata on each side of the central veins.

More challenging are the reddish-green catkins, both male and female on a single tree, each slightly different (see Fig 15). The male catkins are the smaller, tightly packed bobbles (top right in Plate 19) and are worked simply, by creating a series of tiny rounded shapes in green at various angles, interspersed with seed stitches in red. The female catkins present more of a problem. They are shown in close up in Plate 21. Initially, the spherical effect of a collection of round motifs should be worked similarly to the male flowers. Then, using a fine strand of red, work short straight stitches out from each, like tiny starbursts at the centre of the body, and in little fans towards the edge of each cluster.

Additional colour is given to this study by the inclusion of night-scented stocks (*Matthiola bicornis*) and sweet peas (*Lathyrus odoratus*). The pea family is one of the largest genus of flowering plants and is a hugely decorative one for gardeners and embroiderers alike. Apart from the delightful figures which can be described by their coiling tendrils, the flowers are universally attractive, even on those plants which qualify as weeds rather than as respectable garden inhabitants. The tufted vetch (*Vicia cracca*) is a good example (Plate 22).

Vetches are the 'tares' often mentioned in the Bible. In the seventeenth century when the Bible was translated into English, churchgoers would readily have recognized references to the plant which twined and twisted itself through otherwise good crops of barley and oats, strangling them and wreaking havoc at harvest time. An original subject for a pulpit fall could include motifs such as those suggested in Plate 22. The symbolism of good grain is often used in the New Testament (see also Chapter Four) and combined with the arabesques of the vetch an easily repeatable pattern could be achieved, suitable even for an altar frontal (see Fig 16). It would be wise to couch down the long whiskers on the barley and oats, rather than leave them as elongated straight stitches (Plate 22), for the sake of durability, otherwise the various elements of all three plants are small and neat – ideal for such a project.

Both the skylark (*Alauda arvensis*) and the wren (*Troglodytes troglodytes*) share the brown-and-beige colouring of the nightingale, though with more complicated markings, in both cases comprised of speckles, bars and smaller pepper-and-salt freckles. Having successfully captured the simple sweeps of radial stitching needed for the nightingale, for these two birds we must adapt the dalmatian dog technique to convey the larger 'splotches' of colour, together with ticking (see Appendix A, page 126) for the smaller, more delicate striations. Make sure that you have an accurate idea of the angle of the overall sweep of the feathers before working the spots of the dalmation dog work (such as on the head and neck of the skylark) so that the rest of the *opus plumarium* will flow smoothly around them. Take similar care when applying the ticking on a previously worked field of embroidery (for example on the wings of the wren), ensuring that the angle of these small stitches echoes exactly the sweep of the larger area. Both these techniques rely upon maintaining a perfect matching of angles to maintain the realistic effect of the feathers.

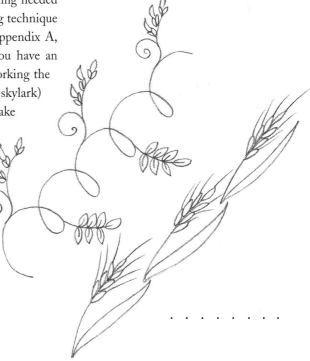

Fig 16 ▷
Sketched on a squared grid (not shown) this
small section of design could be repeated as
often as necessary to cover a large area

HELEN
STEVENS

For such apparently small and insignificant birds, the skylark and the wren both feature strongly in myth, legend and poetry. Perhaps most famously, Shelley's 'To a Skylark' has immortalized that bird, although its pedigree in literature can be traced through Spenser to Shakespeare, Tennyson and Browning. The wren has a rather more chequered past. In a pre-Christian ritual, still remembered as a folk song in Oxfordshire, local rustics hunted and killed a wren once a year to maintain the prosperity of their community. The wren was considered a small but wily bird, once even rivalling the eagle for its position as king of the birds. When a competition was held among all the birds to see who could fly highest, and thus deserve kingship, the eagle soared higher than all the rest, but the tiny wren had perched unseen on his shoulder and, just as the great bird could fly no higher, popped out and claimed the prize.

VIVE L'EMPEREUR

Despite an occasional lapse, such as its oversight of the 'Cutty Wren' (as the folk song calls it), the eagle has always justified its position as an aristocrat among birds. Its image has been used again and again to symbolize magnificence and kingship, from ancient Rome and beyond to Napoleonic France, and still in the emblem of the United States of America, to name but a few. Still more appear as double-headed eagles; eagle feathers are used in ceremonial dress; and the eagle is the symbol of St John the Evangelist. Of all the cyphers of the four Gospel Evangelists – Matthew, a man; Mark, a lion; and Luke, a bull – the eagle of St John seems to be the most easily translated into embroidery and can be used either realistically or in stylized form.

The study in Plate 23 makes a delightful secular miniature, simply framed in a fob-topped miniature frame. It could also be adapted as a central motif for a piece of church embroidery – perfect for a church dedicated to St John the Evangelist. The method of embroidery would be identical, with only the scale changed to suit the final purpose. For this portrait I have chosen a golden eagle (*Aquila chrysaetos*).

Working on a pale background it is essential to shadow line the whole portrait, including all the larger feathers, from the nape of the neck downwards. Careful attention should be paid to the imagined light source and the way in which it will catch the upper and lower feathers (see Fig 17). Work the beak in shades of grey and white in fine split stitch to achieve a slightly matt finish. Similarly the cere, the hardened fleshy yellow area above the beak, and the nostril, should be worked in split stitch. Only when embroidery of the feathers begins should we adopt radial *opus plumarium*, first in very narrow strata, gradually broadening towards the dome of the head and the cheeks. The eye should be worked in a certain order to allow various areas of overlap and give a three-dimensional effect to the head. Work the black pupil first, in perpendicular satin stitch, surrounding it with an arc of chestnut radial stitching, just abutting the black. A fine outline in black split stitch emphasizes the break between the iris and the yellow surround of the eye, which is also worked in linear split stitch (two or more lines of stitching, depending upon

◁ *PLATE 22*

The tiny wren is traditionally referred to in the feminine – Jenny Wren – just as the robin is always male. She is certainly mistress of her chosen haunts, and because of her small size is able to hunt her prey of insects in places inaccessible to other birds. Because no one habitat is essential – rather the ground floor of any habitat – wrens have been recorded in every corner of the British Isles. The ritual seeking of the wren (see text) must have depended to a large extent upon hearing the bird, which is not difficult given that its loud, shrill call is quite out of proportion to its size.

The importance of having a variety of gauges of thread is also evident in this study where the coiling tendrils of the vetch begin in a fine thread and gradually thicken as they progress towards the main stem. Be careful not to leave the 'bump' of a bulky knot showing where you change thickness of thread at various points along each arabesque, and similarly work the 'tails' in neatly on the reverse; on a serpentine design it is simple to work them along the stitches on the reverse of the fabric which effects an invisible finishing-off technique

18.5 x 21cm (7¼ x 8¼in)

Fig 17 ▽
With the imagined light source suggested by the open arrow, each of the larger feathers, even on a miniature study, should be shadow lined individually. The shadow line can be achieved by a series of open straight stitches as shown

your scale). This should be followed by a second outline in black. Only when the eye has been worked can the surrounding feathers fall into place correctly, with those at the top slightly overlaying the eye, giving the typical stern, frowning, eagle-eyed expression.

Work the central vein to each of the larger feathers before going on to work either side of the shaft, lighter above and darker beneath, paying careful attention to the variation in shades. When all the main feathers have been worked, fine details such as the white down peeping out from under the wing joint and the ticking marks on the head and cheek can be added. Where the tiny feathers around the eye overlap the cere, and on the upper throat under the beak, a fine single strand of silk suggests wisps of feathers softening the hard outlines.

Using these techniques the dense quality of the feathers and the harsh horny texture of the beak can be conveyed in close compact stitches which serve the dual purpose of practicality (should the piece be used uncovered in an ecclesiastic setting) together with an ability to convey details built up one over the other, just as in reality.

As a stylized motif, the eagle can be equally attractive and challenging (Plate 24). Loosely adapted from motifs used on a carpet page of the Lindisfarne Gospels, written and illustrated in about AD700, these birds portray all the *joie de vivre* of

PLATE 23 ▷
The noble head of the golden eagle. Its impressive eyesight enables it to spot prey up to 3km (2 miles) distant, and is enhanced by the shade and protection afforded by its heavy brows which also give the bird its stern, disapproving expression. The lethal, hooked beak has given its name to the aquiline nose, once thought to be a characteristic of the nobility. Under the medieval laws of falconry, only a king was allowed to hunt with a golden eagle on his arm. In Britain the golden eagle is confined to the north of Scotland, but it is widespread (though not common) in many other countries of the northern hemisphere. The choice of a brass miniature frame enhances the golden shades of the feathers and a plain creamy background fabric throws the head into relief. Be particularly careful when mounting and framing a single, sharp image such as this that there is no fluff or fragments of thread or fabric left within the frame – they will detract from the overall effect
10.25 x 10.25cm (4 x 4in)
including frame

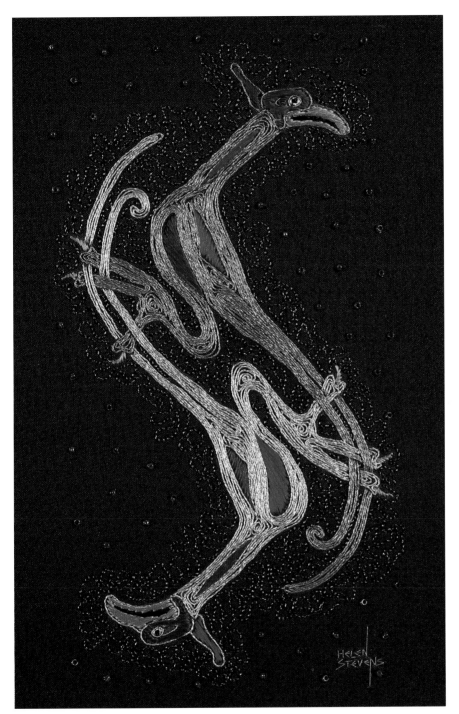

◁ *PLATE 24*
'Ribbon' interlace is a simple term to
discriminate between a design such as this, and
an interlace comprised of just one meandering
or overlapping strand (such as is formed by the
silver thread comprising the sweet pea tendrils
in Plate 19). The interpretation being a
modern one, the thread filling each field of
ribbon 'disappears' behind a ribbon which is
to its forefront, re-emerging on the other side
of the obstacle. Compare this to Plate 27,
part of the ninth-century Maaseik
reconstruction
10.25 x 16cm (4 x 6½in)

Anglo-Saxon illuminated manuscripts. 'Carpet' pages were those pages of a manuscript entirely given over to a (usually) geometric, or repetitive design, normally interlaced and extremely complex. The contemplation of these complicated designs was considered to be an aid to mediation, in much the same way as the 'yantras' of some Eastern religions. Certainly their conversion and working in the embroidered medium is an aid to concentration!

Fig 18 △

*The intricate interlaced designs of the Anglo-
Saxons (this design is inspired by the
Lindisfarne Gospels) is both inspirational and
challenging. Take time to study the pattern of
the interlace before beginning to embroider, and
choose colours carefully so that abutting strands
of the 'ribbon' make a pleasing contrast*

I have treated the main bodies of the eagles as ribbon interlace, and have infilled the fields in surface couched gold and silver thread, using a different metal for each bird to create a continuity of design. The outlines of the heads and beaks have been similarly worked, and then filled with floss silk worked in satin stitch, 'opposite' colourings applied to each bird to continue the quasi-symmetrical effect. These colours have also been allowed to 'flow' into the central cavities of the design, echoing the enamelled effect of Anglo-Saxon jewellery. The claws of each foot are worked in small arcs of stem stitch, thickening towards each toe.

To create the effect of an 'aura' around the motifs, a 2/1T (see page 132, Appendix B) thread has been made using black and gold strands. This has then been couched in a loose, erratic, meandering pattern to about 1.25cm (½in) of the outline of the design, and to fill all areas within the interlace of the motif. Seed beads in a deep green/blue shade have then been stitched evenly, though in a random design, to create an elongated, rectangular field as a base for the whole piece.

The design is worked here on a purple background, suitable for the Lenten season of the Church's year, but could equally well be embroidered on any background colour that does not match any of the main shades of the study itself. By choosing seed beads which are not in sharp contrast to the ground, a change in texture is effected, which means that the design can be worked on a plain fabric background (rather than an expensive figured weave) but still retain a certain richness.

DUCKS AND DRAKES

St Cuthbert, made Bishop of Lindisfarne (today called Holy Island) off the coast of Northumbria in about AD660, is one of the few saints whose name readily emerges in connection with embroidery. Unlike St Dunstan, however, who is known to have been a designer and worker of embroidery (see *The Embroiderer's Countryside*), St Cuthert's association with the art came about after his death when, in around 934, King Athelstan gave a set of three sumptuous embroideries to the Community of St Cuthbert, then resident at Chester-le-Street. The embroideries themselves were probably made at around the turn of the eighth and ninth centuries (at about the same time as the Maaseik embroideries, mentioned on page 46), and made, as their inscription states, to the order of Queen Aelfflaed, Athelstan's stepmother. Later placed in St Cuthbert's coffin, and now on show in the Treasury of Durham Cathedral, along with other relics of the saint, they are perhaps the first, and certainly the finest, extant examples of the type of embroidery which today we might describe as overtly ecclesiastical, with prophets, saints and symbols exquisitely executed but rather posed and lifeless.

St Cuthbert might have felt more at home with the exuberant and amusing motifs of the Maaseik embroideries, which take their cue from nature, for he was a great lover of the natural world and one of its first conservationists. Around the coasts of Northumbria where Cuthbert had made his home (first in the Farne Islands and later at the remote and lonely Lindisfarne) the eider ducks then, as now, bobbed amid the choppy seas, their strange, wistful calls echoing between the waves

◁ *PLATE 25*
Like a middle-aged lady, paddling along
with her petticoats tucked firmly into her
knickers, the eider patrols the waters edge! The
male eider duck's plumage, whilst lacking
colour, has beautifully defined markings which
make it easy to identify among other
wildfowl. The female is much more dowdy.
Both share the deep 'Y'-shaped bill extension
reaching almost to the eye which make the beak
so distinctive. It is thought that this helps to
protect the facial features while the duck
dabbles in rough waters.
Don't be tempted to overstate the number of
birds in flight; a few look natural and
uncontrived, but too many like something from
a Hitchcock film! Often the rule 'less is more'
is a good maxim
14 x 12cm (5½ x 4¾in)

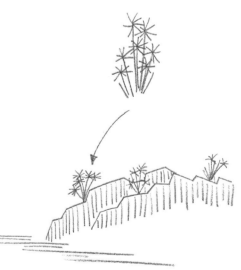

Fig 19 △
Straight stitches can be amazingly 'flexible'
in concept. The thrift, rocks and sea in Plate 25
have all been worked exclusively in
straight stitching, variously angled to create
both outline and substance

and shore. The soft down of the females' underbellies was (and still is) much sought after as a bedding and quilting material and the ducks were persecuted by hunters. St Cuthbert gave them sanctuary, and to this day in the north of England the eider duck is called the Cuddy duck, 'Cuddy' being the diminutive form of Cuthbert. Fortunately, the eider-down is now only removed from nests sparingly and the ducks are no longer in danger.

The male eider duck (*Somateria mollissima*), unlike its more gaudy cousin the mallard drake, has few bright colours to draw it to the attention of hunters, but its call is one of the most evocative to be heard in northern waters. A stocky, sturdy individual (Plate 25), its 'Ooooh-oh, ooooh-oh!' as it rides the waves or paddles in the foreshore is an easy sound to follow. The well-defined areas of brown and white make the eider an easy subject to render in *opus plumarium* and radial stitching, but is a difficult one to place in an appropriate setting – too much colour in the background and the duck will appear insignificant, too little and the whole picture becomes bland and uninteresting. The key is in blending pale and pastel colours with a variety of textures to create a stimulating backdrop and foreground which will throw the main subject into relief without 'drowning' it.

I once lived in the Shetland Islands, and in the brief summers the harsh rocks and crags of the cliffs and rocky outcrops sprang to life with carpets of pink thrift (*Armeria maritima*). Its roots tolerate very high levels of salt in whatever soil is available, and so it can colonize spots that many other plants cannot. On the rocks

PLATE 26 ▷

Everybody's favourite: who can ever forget childhood trips to the park or the river to feed the ducks? And the mallard was almost always first on the scene for rock-hard or soggy bread! The bottle-green of the drake's head is so dark that without the added sheen of sunlight it appears almost black, but when caught in the right light, greens and purples shimmer on the head and flank, transforming a familiar friend into a surprisingly beautiful one.
As with the distant birds in Plate 25, try not to overdo it when adding the gnats: just two or three are an amusing addition. Unlike planning the main setting for the subject, which must be chosen at the drawing-board stage, these little asides can be added freehand at the end of the rest of the embroidery, so wait until the picture is complete before deciding just what to add, and where
12.75 x 12.75cm (5 x 5in)

PLATE 27 ▷

When asked to undertake the research and reconstruct the Maaseik embroideries I did not realize what an ongoing project it was to be. Initially the embroidery was thought to have been an applied decoration, possibly to a costume, but as reconstruction progressed it became evident that it was far too bulky for such a use, and must have had a static purpose. This seems evident, too, by the addition of pearls, possibly added sometime after the original working of the embroideries. They were applied with a single fairly loose thread, and I have tried to replicate their appearance as closely as possible, given that no pearls now remain on the original fragments. Similar compromises had to be made with the gold thread. Originally the gold foil was wrapped around a hair from a horse's tail
Outer dimensions of arcade:
7.5 x 7.5cm (3 x 3in);
height including chevron design top
and bottom: 8.5cm (3½in)

in the background of Plate 25 it has been impressionistically suggested in silk, straight stitches (long for stems and leaves and worked in tiny sunbursts for the flowers) emerging from closely worked ranks of perpendicular stitching in cotton, shaded and shadowed, to create the rough, jagged surface of the rocks. In the foreground, similarly worked smaller rocks are surmounted by seaweed, its fronds couched in a meandering floss silk thread, loosely worked along a central vein. The water presents a third texture: densely worked horizontal straight stitching in a fine, but twisted, silk thread. These three features, snugly surrounding the main subject, present a pleasing whole.

Seabirds wheel overhead to give added movement to the picture. These can be simply and effectively worked in a fine strand of silk, or similarly narrow-gauged thread (as described in Fig 52, Chapter Six, page 106).When working on a pale background, be careful when beginning and ending your stitches on a very delicate motif such as a distant bird. Whip the thread into the stitches on the reverse of the embroidery, taking several 'winds' through them, if necessary, and snip the end off as close as possible to the work itself, leaving no 'tails' which might show through the fine fabric.

With the more colourful mallard drake (*Anas platyrhynchos*) it is equally as important to pick a complementary setting, rather more vibrant, to balance the main subject (Plate 26). The rosebay willowherb (*Epilobium angustifolium*) has pretty pink flowers and rhubarb-red buds, whilst the bulrushes' (*Typha latifolia*) deep-brown heads echo the brown of the duck's breast. Both plants have a tall upright habit, which curve elegantly. These two plants are roughly symmetrical, with the duck effectively framed between the two, allowing for spontaneity in the application of the grasses and water at the base of the design. Again, a little added movement has been achieved by gnats dancing overhead. Each of these is formed by working two tiny lazy-daisy stitches as wings, above a few randomly straight-stitched legs.

Ducks always seem to hold a special place in our hearts: who can forget Jemima Puddleduck and her companions waddling away from Tom Kitten? Their amusing nature as a motif did not escape the creator of the Maaseik embroideries, who placed a pair of them looking longingly up into a tree of life (Plate 27). As in our contemporary study of the mallard, a rough symmetry has been achieved in this visual 'joke', as the left-hand bird is clearly placed in front of the tree, whilst the duck to the right is placed behind the branch which balances the tree's form. This bird reaches up toward a trefoil leaf, while the other has clearly missed his mark.

Amusing and entertaining as these motifs may be, they were still sumptuous and richly adorned. Once the gold and silkwork has been completed, as shown in Plate 18, Chapter One, pearls were added to further enhance the design. These were used chiefly to outline the various integral parts of the design, and in particular to designate the areas which were to be 'read', the arcades, as opposed to the supporting embroidery. The seeds beads applied to the stylized eagle study in Plate 24 achieve the same ends, drawing the eye towards the dominant pattern.

Fig 20 △
The willowherb family create attractive and useful motifs both in the distance and in close up. To the left is the rosebay willowherb featured in Plate 26. Right, the great willowherb presents a different outline, fuller and less tapering than its cousin (see Plate 30)

CHAPTER THREE

EARTH, WIND AND WATER

Up the airy mountain, down the rushy glen
We daren't go a-hunting for fear of little men ...
Some in the reeds of the black mountain-lake
With frogs for their watchdogs, all night awake.

The Fairies
William Allingham, 1850

HE fire crackled, sending a spray of sparks towards the rafters, wafting up like a dragon's breath. The nobles dozed on their benches and my Lord retired to his chamber. The Story-teller's voice was low:

'*Truly, the threads which 'broider the fabric of life reveal many a truth, but they also hide many a secret. Long ago in the ancient West, Bran, the son of Febal, met a beautiful woman amid the spring blossoms of silver and white. She was clothed in silks the like of which neither he nor his followers had ever seen, decorated as if by the needles of the gods. She sang to them of a land far away over the seas where happiness was the lot of all heroes, where all the women were as magical as she, and sorrow, sickness and death were unknown; and then she vanished in a rustle of fine samite. Bran took ship and sailed further west than any man had gone before, encountering many strange visions and adventures. Finally he reached the Island of Beautiful Women, where the lovely stranger awaited him, and called him ashore, but he was afraid to land in the rough waters. She threw him a ball of thread, similar to her dress, so beautiful that it took his breath away. It stuck to his hand and by magic the ship was drawn to land, where it and its crew were bound by the threads of enchantment. The isle was so delightful that time almost stood still; when it seemed that only a year had passed, in fact many centuries had gone by, and when the voyagers returned home they were old men, only remembered in fables.*'

PLATE 29 △

'*T*' *The pedigree of this lovely little dragon is a mixture of the Oriental and the Anglo-Saxon. A dragon with four legs usually indicates Chinese breeding, but he must have Western blood too, for his overall body shape is far more Occidental than Eastern! Worked simply in satin and directional stitching, his outline has not been confused with shadowing; the alternating sweeps of stitching are sufficient to give a change of shade to the gold silk as the light catches it at differing angles. His fiery breath is suggested by the red and gold of the letter T. Working on a shiny satin-like background achieves a rich effect, but care must be taken that fine enough needles are used. Too broad an eye will make holes impossible to disguise*
8.75 x 12cm (3½ x 4¾in)

HERE BE DRAGONS

There is something in most of us which revels in a good fairy story. Children love to hear the same tales over and over again – woe betide the teller if elements are changed without permission – and as adults recurring images, perhaps differently couched, but still essentially the same, strike deep chords in our consciousness. Which of us has not been tempted to give that old lamp a rub, make three wishes, maybe even kiss that frog – just in case!

There are times in embroidery, too, when we are overcome by a desire to create something familiar, something often worked before, and yet give it a fantastic edge, an opening into the surreal, even the supernatural; ultimately to achieve a unique piece of work, at the same time adhering to established traditions and cultures.

It is impossible to think of Chinese embroidery without associating it with dragons, but why should our dragons imitate theirs? The cover illustration (also shown in Plate 30) draws upon Celtic and Viking design to conjure up two splendid 'wormes', and then draws us through the smokescreen of the imagination to the real world, where dragonflies are quite as wonderful as their namesakes. Before taking that step, however, it might be useful to look at some techniques which can make the natural world seem as magical as its parallel universe.

Although working on a black background does not prevent us from being entirely accurate in our naturalistic studies, it immediately gives scope for the addition of a slightly heightened awareness of light, colour and movement. In Plate 28 movement is everywhere. Above the water line a stiff breeze carries droplets of water from recently dipped leaves and flowers away to the right; immediately below the surface a strong current sweeps everything along in its path; while on the river bed the upper currents create eddies which swirl the weeds and water insects back and forth. The whole study is a shifting mass of motifs, and we have been able to emphasize the environment of the water by the use of silver thread, blue strands of cellophane and startling ice-blue silk, all of which would have presented little impact on a pale background.

The frog is clearly aiming for his lily-pad. This is made obvious by highlighting his eye in a direct alignment with his objective (see Fig 21), but the stream of bubbles which rises towards the surface pose a problem – will the current carry him away? Using a very fine strand of silver thread, small circles have been couched down, some randomly filled with ice-blue silk. Tiny tear-drop motifs in the same silver thread have been worked in satin stitch to describe the wind-blown water, and a thicker gauge of the same silver has been couched around the lower outlines of the frog to delineate his body. Gold thread has been used on the upper surfaces. Uncut stones of aquamarine, aventurine and rose quartz are loosely stitched over a meandering couched thread of two-tone chenille to give a three-dimensional quality to the river bed.

Turning to our dragon/dragonfly study, we can use some of the same ideas. The fantastic elements of the design are worked in metal threads, and vibrant, enamel-like shades of colour. A ribbon interlace forms the bodies of the dragons,

◁ *PLATE 28 (page 48 – 49)*
Where do fairy tales come from? Many, of course, are the distorted folk memories of long-lost rituals and religious beliefs, but surely some must have been inspired by the natural world. The careless princess who played with a golden ball at the river's edge, dropped it in the water and had it returned by a kindly frog (a prince, of course, under a curse!) might well have been the invention of some doting father whose little girl was entranced by the golden ball of the yellow water-lily flower (Nuphar lutea), *for it looks very like a plaything as it bobs above the surface. The plant is immortalized in stone in Westminster Abbey, carved in the roof bosses, possibly to encourage celibacy, as it was said to be a 'destroyer of passion' in Classical times.*

The river water-crowfoot (Ranunculus fluitans), *on the other hand, was considered a troublesome weed, hindering the passage of boats with its thick, vigorous growth.*

The common frog (Rana temporaria) *is sadly not as common as it once was. Virus, low rainfall and pollution have all taken their toll, but for all that between January and March, when pairing, it is not unusual to hear the male's wistful, buzzing croak beside shallow ponds. In colour they range in shades of mottled yellow, green and brown, the females larger than the males. To create a smooth, moist appearance to the skin, several stands of floss silk have been used together in a loose 3 or 4/1F thread. Brown dalmatian dog spots blend evenly with the surrounding green. The membranes between the long toes of the back feet are in a single strand of silk, outlined in metallic silver, giving way to gold where the light from above reflects the green/gold of the watery environment*

Embroidery shown life-size:
42 x 28cm (16½ x 11in)

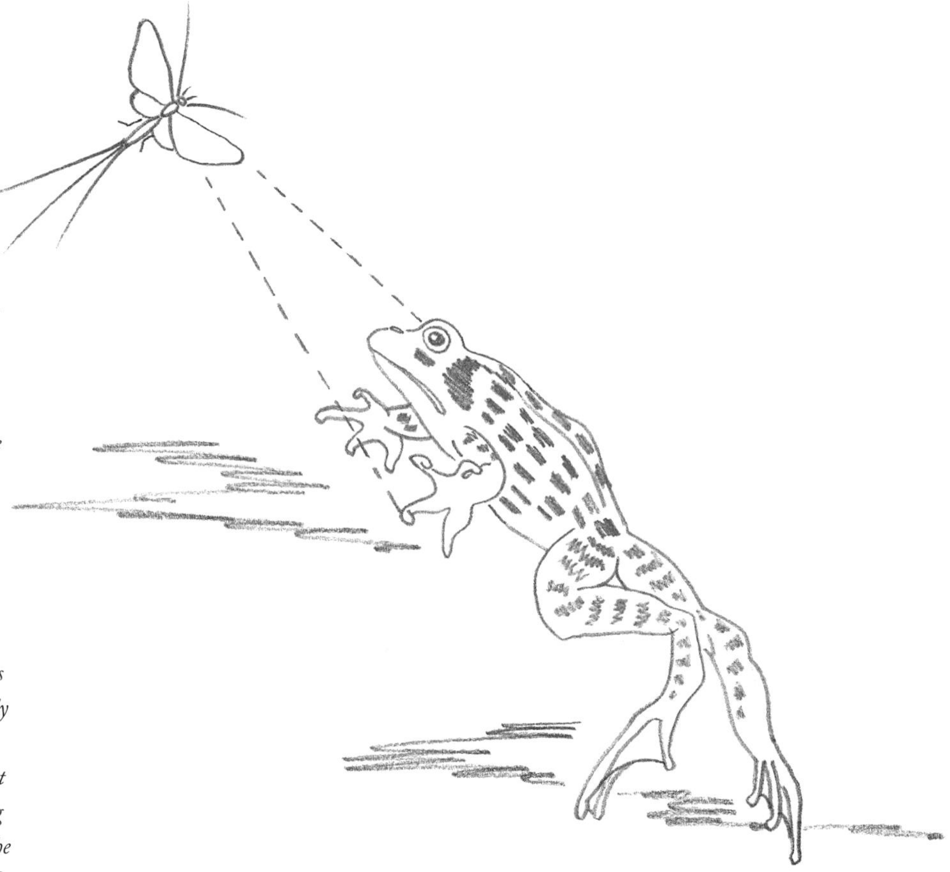

Fig 21 ▷

To give the impression that a subject's interest is really focused on a particular motif, draw a bead between the eye of the onlooker and some other part of its body, positioning the object of interest where the two lines intersect. Here, the frog's eye and near front leg are the 'viewfinders'. Emphasize the effect by highlighting the eye towards the motif in question

PLATE 30 ▷

The emperor dragonfly (Anax imperator) *is certainly king of the water's edge. It is fiercely territorial, and a male intruding upon a rival's air space will almost certainly prompt an aerial dog fight, resulting in wings being torn apart, occasionally with fatal results. The emperor is also a tenacious hunter, hawking for its prey among other flying insects, including smaller members of its own species. Perhaps it was these belligerent tendencies, together with its magnificent appearance, which prompted its coupling with the dragons of legend.*
The two 'contending dragons' of the sky, facing each other, were said in many cultures to typify all complements and opposites, the celestial and terrestrial powers of the universe – yin and yang (see Fig 27, page 63). Forming the gateway to and from the otherworld, here they frame the white water-lily (Nymphaea alba) *and great willowherb* (Epilobium hirsutum). *The beauty of the white water-lily is reflected in some if its localized names, such as swan among the flowers and lady of the lake. It is the flower of the Great Mother goddess in the waters 'wherein existence comes to be and passes away'. The lotus as a stylized Egyptian motif will be explored more fully in Chapter Six*
Embroidery shown life-size:
23 x 30.5cm (9 x 12in)

the silkwork in snake stitch, outlined in couched gold and silver. The Chinese believe that their dragons come to life only then the white highlight is added to the eye, and here the highlights give the impression of the twin dragons' eye-to-eye contact. We enter the magical world of nature through an arch created by the smoke of their breath. Once there, we witness the emperor dragonfly skimming over the mystical lotus flower towards a familiar wildflower of the wayside, the willowherb. It is as if we have taken an epic journey and returned to our starting point.

OVER THE WATER

Whilst all is activity under the waters of the 'rushy glen', there is no lack of colour and enchantment above the surface. Plate 31 captures a tumbling, racing stream as it meanders down from the peaks of the Cumbrian hills, through rocky outcrops, water plants and heathland. As the heather begins to bloom on the distant hillsides the colours are breathtaking, and yet unlike the complex, multi-disciplined work necessary to create the underwater scene, this landscape can be simply worked, its splendours uncomplicated by special effects.

Horizontal straight stitching is a technique which is elementary, but requires practice if it is to be used effectively. Colours may be blended smoothly or terminate sharply depending on the desired effect, and it is important to understand the

PLATE 31 ▷

In a study such as this, where the distant hills
and foreground are so full of vibrancy and
colour, a mere suggestion of the sky is enough to
convey the idea of far distance above and
beyond the hills. Using the finest silk possible,
and lightening the shade of blue towards the
horizon, long straight stitches echo the
patchwork of the hills
26.75 x 21.5cm (10 x 8½in)

Fig 22 ▽

Use a void between hills and other distant
planes of perspective to create an impression of
their separate identity (a). Where colours or
shades change within a specific plane, blend
them smoothly along an imagined cut-off point
as indicated by the hatched lines (b)

process of sketching the landscape if we are to create these impressions effectively. The illusion of depth in a study such as this, where the background hills recede gently, can be created by leaving a void between each 'dimension' (Fig 22a), at which points juxtaposed colours will be abruptly cut off from one another (even if they are the same shade). Within each individual dimension, colours will meld together evenly, with stitches taken into each other so that the shades may change, but the identity of each hill remains separate (Fig 22b). When a foreground or middle-distance feature breaks the horizontal stitching, a very narrow 'halo' of unstitched fabric should remain around it, giving a feeling of space between the tree and the hill, the rocks and the sweeping foreground, and so on. These ideas are explored in greater depth in *The Embroiderer's Country Album*.

Trees and bushes are worked first in their skeletal shapes, and then clothed with fine seed stitching to create their leaves. When all the foreground landscape is complete, grasses, in the shape of perpendicular straight stitches, are worked over the top of water and heath along the river bank. At the edge of the stream the jaunty little dipper (*Cinclus cinclus*) begins its descent into the water. Unique among birds, the dipper seeks its food by walking underwater, patrolling the river bed for insects, worms and tadpoles. The 'little men' spotted along the streams of northern Britain, often wearing green jackets or feathers, are usually referred to as sprites, elves or Brownies. It does not require an enormous leap of the imagination to see their likeness in the frogs and birds that frequent those waters.

The rough grassy fells of northern England are home to the wild liquorice (*Ononis repens*), once called 'cammock' (Plate 32). It was thought to be a tool of mischievous fairies who, perhaps having a grudge against a farmer or his wife, would

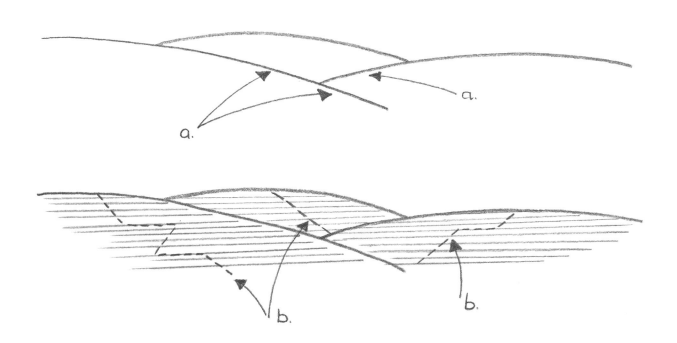

PLATE 32 ▷

*Unlike butterflies 'clubbed' antennae, those of
moths often have a feathery appearance. Their
bodies, too, are furry compared to the brittle
bodies of butterflies, and their wings softer and
more textured, without the shimmering,
reflective scales of their day-flying cousins. As a
rule, all these effects can be achieved by using
shorter stitches than would otherwise be
employed – often a necessity because of their
complex shadings (see Fig 23)
8 x 8.5cm (3 x 3¹⁄₄in)*

Fig 23 ▽

*The Kentish glory. A complicated motif such
as this can be worked easily if the correct order
of working is followed:
The crescent on the upper wings is worked
first. From the inside of each wing build up
the strata of colours, blending them smoothly
into each other and into the crescent. Next,
the smaller crescents at the very edges of the
upper wings are worked in white, the
surrounding buff colour blended around them.
Finally, work the lower wings (spots first)
and the body, allowing the rounded contours
of the abdomen and so on to disguise the
inner edges of the wings*

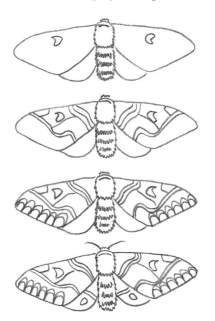

use it to turn the milk sour and taint the butter and cheese. Its deep, matted roots
also tangled in horse-drawn ploughshares, giving it another name: restharrow,
meaning literally to 'stop the harrow'. Children loved it, however, as the roots tasted
of sweet liquorice, and many a saucer of milk was left out for the Brownies in
exchange for this natural treat. Heathland is also the home of the Kentish glory
(*Endromis versicolora*), once common, but now only found in parts of Scotland. The
combination of these two subjects makes a pretty picture. Worked on a peachy
background, the pastel-pink of the flowers and the apricot, beige and browns of the
moth combine to bring a breath of summer on the high moors. Silver-greens work
equally well here as on a black background, but it is important to shadow line each
leaf carefully to emphasize the soft, serrated edges of the young growth.

The upper wings of the moth bear complicated motifs, and it is essential that
they should be clearly drawn and transferred onto your fabric (see Appendix B,
page 133). With an accurate outline it is possible to concentrate upon choosing the
correct colouring and blending the nine or so strata of the shades smoothly, one at
a time, not overlooking the inclusion of the distinctive crescent moon on each upper
wing in dalmatian dog technique (see Fig 23).

In a different setting similar colours can create an entirely different atmosphere.
The milk-chocolate browns of the Kentish glory, together with only a different
shade of green, can summon up the sparkling chill of snowdrops and the last
snowfall of the season (Plate 33).

When I was a child, the crisp rustle of a dead leaf as it blew along the road was always the scurrying of the snowdrop fairy. She had once been dressmaker to the Queen of the Fairies, but some misunderstanding had placed her under a curse, and each year she became smaller and smaller. Eventually she became so tiny that the only clothes she could fashion were the white bonnets worn by the snowdrops. Each January when their pretty heads bob in the breeze I wonder what happened to her!

◁ *Fig 24*

To create differing curves on the antennae of moths, work the feathery filaments in opposing orders. To the left a concave pair of antennae has the lower edges worked first, followed by the upper. To the right, a convex pair is worked conversely: upper first, followed by lower

◁ *PLATE 33*

There are many types of snow – the Eskimo peoples have up to forty different words to describe it – but even we recognize the difference between the large fluffy flakes of a prolonged snowfall, the soft, delicate snowflakes of a late winter shower and the icy crystals of a really bitter snap. Those shown here are of the second variety. Gently settling on upper surfaces but not guaranteed to last, areas on the ground are already beginning to melt into undulating, icy water, straight stitches in the non-cellophane strand of a blending filament. In Plate 66, Chapter Six we take a look at using sequins and beads to create a completely different effect.

Snowdrops (a more vivid local name is the 'snow-piercer') are scattered throughout England, Wales and southern Scotland. At the Feast of the Purification of St Mary, on February 2nd, village girls would pick bunches of the flowers and wear them as symbols of purity, hence another name 'the fair maid of February'. Its generic name Galanthus *is derived from two Greek words for 'milk' and 'flower'. Blue-green leaves are worked in snake stitch, the paler green stems in narrow stem stitch and the nodding petals and buds in carefully chosen directional stitching. Undersides of the petals are worked in pale grey thread to suggest that they are in a slight shadow*
9.75 x 11.5cm (3³/₄ x 4¹/₂in)

Fig 25 ▷

*Differing effects on the same leaf motif can
be created by changing their surroundings.
The topmost motif appears to lie on the ground:
shading in and around the main leaves
suggests that their background is close and
dense. These two leaves shown in the lower
design are apparently lifted by the lack of
shading behind them. Added interest can then
be created by grasses seeming to grow through
the tattered holes*

Unlike the scene in Plate 28, where the breeze carries all before it, there is no breath of wind here. The snowflakes – tiny sunbursts of straight stitches, interspersed with speckles of silver thread – fall softly and dust the upper surfaces of each feature in seed stitches of pure white cotton. There is no overall 'direction' in the picture to suggest sideways movement, just the fluttering of the snowflakes, and the otherwise motionless quality is emphasized by the grasses growing up through torn dead leaves. Compare the differences in light and shade, stillness and movement as illustrated in Plates 32, 33 and 35.

DABBERLOCKS AND FURBELOWS

We need not venture into the realms of the unknown to encounter the strangest of names. The underwater world seems to attract the oddest, and most descriptive, names for its inhabitants. The low-growing water weeds at the bottom of Plate 28 are rigid hornwort (*Ceratophyllum denersum*) and the beautifully descriptive slender naiad (*Najas flexilis*) – in Classical mythology the naiads were water nymphs. In Plate 34 we venture into salt water to meet the *Aurelia aurita*, also known as the 'frilly lady' or, more often, the common jellyfish. Frilly ladies are found all around the coast of Britain, and one late summer evening in the beautiful little fishing village of St Abbs on the east coast of Scotland, when the water was as clear as crystal, I was fortunate enough to see a swarm of them moving slowly through the harbour entrance. The umbrella-shaped body, or bell, contracts slowly, expelling water and propelling the animal along. Small fish and crustaceans brush against the numerous tiny waving tentacles below the bell, are stunned and then pushed into the central mouth by the large, more mobile tentacles. However, these are no *femme fatales* as far as humans are concerned; the sting is rarely strong enough to be painful to anything larger than a prawn.

The use of cellophane thread has here been extended from its ability to convey a watery effect into the body of the jellyfish itself. First, however, the nebulous bell

PLATE 34 ▷

*Eel grass, bootlace weed and many other small
varieties of seaweed can be slightly stylized to
create an attractive and useful motif to soften
an otherwise stark area of the design, such as at
the foot of the dabberlocks. In floating
embroidery, it is possible to lengthen or shorten
the fronds by varying the length of the
loop of thread held away from the fabric during
working. Once anchored the loops may be
arranged to suit the design, either falling back
against the fabric haphazardly, or blown to one
side to suggest eddies of wind or water. Take
great care when handling your embroidery
after this technique has been worked,
as it is easy to catch the loose threads and pull
them disastrously out of shape. It is wise
to carry out this stitch as the very last task
before mounting and framing your work
(see Appendix B)*
16.5 x 30.5cm (6½ x 12in)

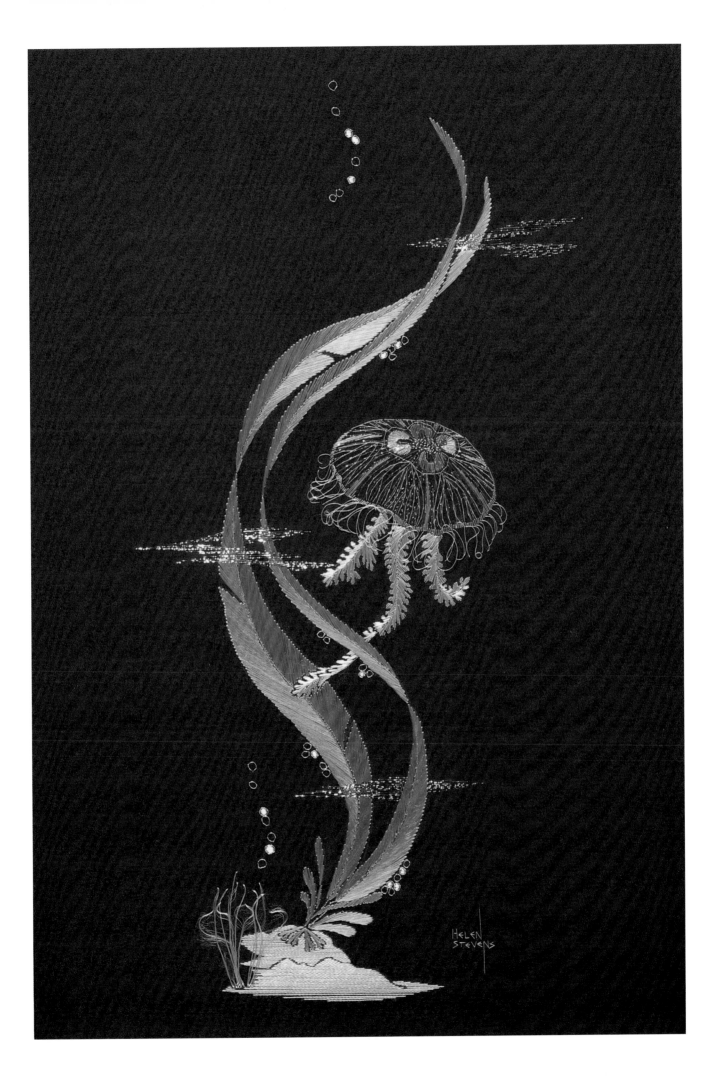

has been embroidered in a single strand of silk, delineating the four pale-violet horseshoe-shaped reproductive organs at the centre of the animal and the 'struts' of the umbrella-like body. Then the lacy veins are worked in an even finer gauge of silk – in white – and finally the whole is overlaid with a rainbow-coloured cellophane strand separated from a blending filament. These filaments are now available in a wide range of colours and thickness; it is generally better to opt for the finest, and use the cellophane strand singly, in long straight stitches, worked quite close together.

The long frilly tentacles which give the lady her name are worked in fine radial stitching, slipping down the central vein of each ribbon, and finally the stinging tentacles are worked in the finest gauge of white silk, overlaying other features by the use of floating embroidery (Appendix A, page 129). The same device as in Plate 28 has been used to create rising bubbles.

Seaweeds are marvellous motifs, but require us to learn a whole new vocabulary. In Plate 34, the frilly lady drifts through two fronds – not leaves – of dabberlocks (*Alaria esculenta*). Its central vein is a midrib, here worked in surface couched gold thread, which gives way to the 'stipe', from which grow elegant little paisley-shaped 'leaflets' (the plant's reproductive organs). Beneath them is the 'holdfast' which anchors the seaweed to a rock. Both the leaflets and the holdfast are worked in carefully angled directional stitching, as are both sides of each frond, which often split down to the midrib, giving a torn appearance.

A relative of the dabberlock – another kelp – is the furbelow (*Saccorhiza ployschides*), taking its name from (or perhaps giving it to) fabric flounces and trimmings. It is also known as mermaids' locks (see Fig 26). Both names are highly appropriate, and whilst she is not a mermaid, the fairy in Plate 35 was inspired by its billowing mass. Bellbine (*Calystegia sepium*) is a common plant of seaside lanes, scrambling up to 3m (10ft) high in hedgerows tossed by coastal winds. Also known as hedge bindweed, its tough, sinewy stems coil anticlockwise around supporting plants, but its large showy trumpets often thrust their heads up above its host to crown hedges in shimmering white.

The fragile body of the wind fairy has been worked in the same technique as her sister in Plate 15, page 29. The mass of

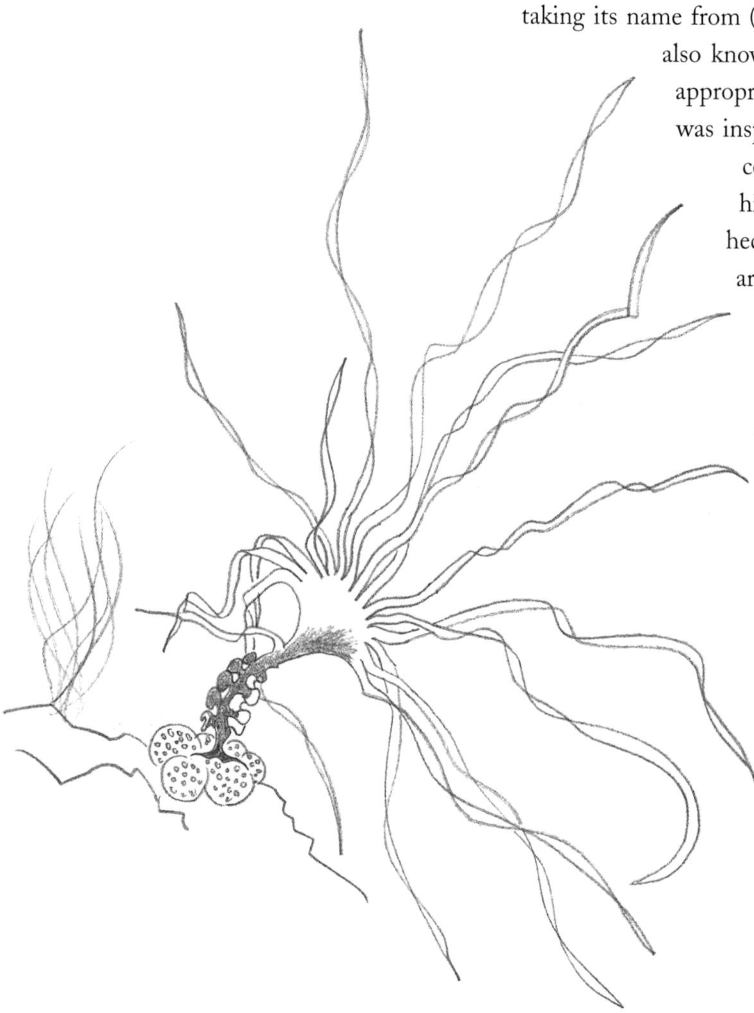

◁ *Fig 26*
*The fabulously shaped furbelow suggests all
sorts of possibilities in the design of underwater
embroideries. Like the dabberlock in Plate 34
careful attention would have to be paid to the
directional stitching of each frond. Water
currents billow the plant to the right,
suggesting movement in the same way as the
breeze in Plate 35 carries away the real
wind fairy's hair*

HELEN
STEVENS

◁ *PLATE 35*

*In common with any other fine motif, take care
when beginning and ending tiny subjects such
as flying feathers or dandelion parachutes that
the threads on the reverse of the fabric do not
show through and ruin the outline of your
work. Always complete each motif separately;
never jump from one to the next.
The holly blue butterfly (Celastrina argiolus)
is a common sight along coastal paths and
hedgerows in southern England, easily
identifiable by the black-and-white bordered
wing markings. The main blue strata of the
wing should be worked first, then the two
narrow bands added, smoothly blending into
one another. One of the simplest of all wing
patterns, it is still one of the prettiest, perhaps
because it speaks to us of long hot summer days*
13 x 14cm (5 x 5½in)

fine hair is snatched by the sea breeze and blown to the right, the wind emphasized
by the tiny feathers and dandelion seeds caught up in it, and the other elements of
the picture – the blue butterfly, the trumpet of the flower – all incline in the same
direction to maintain the illusion, similar to the devices used in Plate 28.

The versatility of the cellophane blending filaments is shown again in this
study, where an ice-blue strand has been separated and used to enhance the
underside of the fairy's butterfly wings. The dull brown, mottled markings actually
found on the underside of the peacock butterfly seemed inappropriate to this
setting, and so a little artistic licence was employed!

Nature presents us with many challenges in the shape of insect wings, from
the complex structure of the dragonfly (Plate 30) worked in honeycomb stitch –
fully described in Appendix A – to the soft sheen of moths, vibrant shimmer of
butterflies and rapid whirr of bumble bees. Though we tend to think of them as
crawling insects many beetles are agile flyers and, in flight, make unusual subjects
(Plates 4 and 10). As well as the wings themselves, the wing cases must be carefully
worked, in proportion to the insect, balancing the motifs. Plate 36 is a detail of
Plate 4, showing glow-worms as they approach apple blossom. The beauty of the
glow-worm is in its light and its elegant, hovering flight – they are not spectacular

insects in themselves. Worked in shades of gold and brown, however, with the addition of fine gold metallic thread, they are charming. The wings have been simply worked in straight stitches similar to those of bees (see Chapter Four). Yet another application has been found for the use of split blending filament; here it suggests light shimmering off the reflective bodies of the insects.

Plate 37 brings together many of the aspects of work which have been examined in this chapter. Above and below the water line there is movement, and it is even carried through the surface tension, as a droplet of water from a wet leaf plops down, creating in turn two tiny upward splashes. The delicate heads of the flowers are dancing in a light, changeable breeze, shaking loose recently fallen raindrops; they are attended by mayflies, their straight, simple wings contrasting the complicated form of the dragonfly's honeycomb structure and vibrant body colour. Tiny daphnia swim underwater; the eye of the fish is drawn towards them, while striate cellophane stitching criss-crosses its body. At the very foot of the design, the simple stony river bed is enlivened by floating embroidery in the shape of water weeds. There is balance and harmony – true yin and yang.

PLATE 36 (detail of Plate 4) ▷
Apple-blossom time, spring weddings and maypoles on the village green - all seem to conjure up the image of 'Olde England'. There can be no prettier blossom than that of the apple tree, whether the wild crab or the many cultivated varieties. Old favourites like orchard Codlins and Pippins are perhaps the most attractive, their honeysuckle-sweet fragrance attracting a wide variety of insects. Worked on a black background their pale pastel pink-and-white petals need nothing to enhance their natural beauty, save a specking of yellow silk at the centre of each – the pollen-rich anthers.
The apple blossom and fruit is the 'silver bough' of the Celtic otherworld and is said to have magical powers. In many versions of the story at the opening of this chapter Bran is given a mystical silver branch by his mystical mistress, tempting him to undertake his long voyage to her island
10.25 x 13cm (4 x 5in)

◁ *PLATE 37*

*Long ago in medieval Germany, so the legend
says, a knight and his lady strolled by a river.
The knight stooped to pick a bunch of flowers
for his beloved and, overbalanced by the
weight of his armour, fell into the stream.
Drowning, he threw the posy to his lady and
cried* 'Vergisz mein nicht!' – 'Forget me not!'
*From this romantic event the delicate little
blue-and-white water forget-me-not*
(Myosotis scorpioides) *derives its name.
The tale is immortalized by Samuel Taylor
Coleridge in his poem* The Keepsake.
Water-plantain (Alisma plantago-aquatica)
*attracts many insects to its pretty dancing
flowers, which each produce several drops of
sweet nectar at the base of their stamens. Flies
visit each in turn helping to pollinate the
plants. Three-petalled flowers are unusual; the
water-plantain is no relation to other
plantains (the shape of its leaf misled
botanists of earlier centuries), and its only
relation is the arrowhead.
Both flowers are worked in simple radial
stitching, bright sunlit colours vibrant against
a black background*
13 x 25.5cm (5 x 10in)

Fig 27 △
*The Yin-Yang symbol (also known as Tai Chi)
represents the balance of all things necessary to
produce the tangible world. Each half carries
the seed of the other within itself: light and
dark; male and female; good and evil; each is
counterbalanced to achieve harmony*

CHAPTER FOUR

PLANTLORE

Tell her to make me a cambric shirt,
Parsley, sage, rosemary and thyme,
With neither seam nor fine needlework,
Then she'll be a true love of mine

Traditional

AGAIN my Lady's eyes were fastened upon her embroidery. The night had grown quiet and the warmth of the fire had brought out the perfume of the dried herbs strewn upon the floor. She smiled up at the Story-teller:

'*You speak as if you thought all threads were spun of mischief – but there are many which tell only of beauty and fruitfulness. Long ago when the Earth Mother was worshipped in our villages she was borne from field to field in a wain covered by a sacred hanging embroidered with herbs of gold; the cloth only had to brush the hedgerow of a meadow and it would be fruitful for a whole year. The pious were buried with fragments of the cloth to protect them into the next world, and even today the priest intones chants from that time (though perhaps, being a man, he knows it not!), while at harvest we dress the fairest maid in a gown of green stitched with flowers and leaves and reverence her. Then our needles wield threads of pure magic! And on the sixth day of every week my mother taught me to remember the goddess Frigg, a wife of Odin, and queen of the night sky. From her distaff she spun long pearly webs of cloud which shone in the heavens. The starry constellations of her spinning wheel and of her covered wagon would guide home any traveller who called upon her name. But I must be still, or I shall give away too many women's secrets!*'

PLATE 39 △
'*A*' *According to legend, spotted medick (Medicago arabica) was once simple clover, growing at the foot of the Cross. Drops of Christ's blood falling on the plant gave it its characteristic spots, and also its popular name of 'Christ's clover'. Its attractive scrolling design would work well as an overall repeat design on church vestments, and is here combined with tiny roughly cut peridot stones, traditionally used to ward off anger and jealousy, and to help control those emotions*
9 x 12.25cm (3½ x 5in)

SCARBOROUGH FAIR

Parsley, sage, rosemary and thyme – a combination of herbs which trips off the tongue with a sound as sweet as the lazy buzzing of the bumble bees attracted to their pollen-rich flowers. All four herbs have magical associations, and in each verse of the old folk song the mystical completion of an impossible task suggests that only by overcoming such adversity is true love really attained – the impossibility, for instance, of making a shirt without seam or needlework.

Plantlore, wortcunning, or simply the use of herbs for elementary medicinal purposes, and its representation in embroidery, is as old as mankind itself. The efficacy of the cures could be enhanced by astrological associations, chants and charms, and the binding of herbs with threads; the 'three-times-three' binding of a posy with cord is still thought by some to add love-magic to a bouquet. Medicinal and culinary herbs tend to have a delicacy of form and feature which lends itself well to embroidery, whether in a detailed lifelike study such as that in Plate 38, or as the simple individual sprigs so popular on the cottons and muslins of the Regency and Georgian periods (see Fig 28). The language of flowers, so loved by the Victorians, adds another dimension to their imagery which far pre-dates nineteenth-century sentimentalism. Shakespeare's *Ophelia* in Hamlet gives rosemary – '... that's for remembrance' – which together with the remaining three from the Scarborough Fair quartet – representing festivity, ability and activity – begin to give an insight into the reasons for their choice as chorus in this ancient song. Similar herbs and grasses would have been ritually stitched into the covering of the Lady's wain, pulled from field to field to ensure fertility and embroidered on the costume of the May Queen as an incarnation of the Mother Goddess – the '*Greensleeves*' of the old Tudor madrigal.

The familiar curled parsley (*Petroselinum crispum* – bottom left in Plate 38) was brought to Britain from the Mediterranean in the Middle Ages. Its straight-leafed cousin (far left) was used by the Romans centuries earlier, and although considered native, was originally an ancient Greek herb, regarded as both medicinal and sacred. According to folklore, it should always be grown from a seed planted on Good Friday (in common with many plants associated with Christ's passion, see Plate 39) and should never be transplanted. The simple, centrally veined, spear-shaped leaves of the straight variety present no problems in embroidery, but the deep, curly, frilled leaves of the garden cultivar are a challenge. Tightly clustered and whorled around themselves, it is impossible to see the veins of the leaves, and so

⊲ PLATE 38 (page 64 – 65)
Bumble bees buzzing in the herb bed – there can be no more atmospheric sound of summer. Aerodynamically it is a mystery how the bumble bee flies, as its bodyweight should be too heavy for its wings. The resulting frenetic activity of those small wings, beating furiously to keep the bee airborne, produces the characteristic loud, droning buzz. To capture the essence of that movement in a static medium such as embroidery necessitates some subtle special effects. Work the wings in long, radiating, straight stitches, but allow some of the background fabric to show through the stitching, even in the areas which overlay the body of the insect (Fig 32). In this way a 'subliminal' message is sent to the eye that there is movement and 'air' between the stitches. It also suggests the diaphanous, transparent texture of the wings, which is still evident when the bee is at rest, centre and bottom right
Embroidery shown life-size:
37 x 28cm (14¹/₂ x 11in)

Fig 28 ▷
Simplified, slightly stylized motifs make pleasing sprigs which could be used as an all-over carpet design suitable for a panel of embroidery, or scattered randomly to create a more open design. Clockwise from the top: lavender, wild parsley and camomile

the structure must be suggested by contrasting light and dark shades of green to suggest the lower and upper surfaces of each leaf respectively (see Plate 40). Careful shadow lining both on the fleshy stems and leaves is important to enhance the effect of depth, arcs of *opus plumarium* and, where a rosette of foliage faces the onlooker, rotating radial stitching by a full 360 degrees completes the illusion of a bushy, three-dimensional pompon. Similar techniques are needed to create the head of the cornflower in Plate 44 (see page 76).

Both sage (*Salvia officinalis*) and rosemary (*Rosmarinus officinalis*) share the delicate two-lipped flower-heads so typical of aromatic herbs. They are quite a complicated structure but, once analyzed, can be translated fairly easily into embroidery (see Fig 29). Depending upon the size of the subject and the scale of the embroidery the anther-bearing stamens can either be included, as with the sage, or omitted as in the case of the rosemary, allowing the tiny pollen bodies to dance freely around the flower-head.

PLATE 40 (detail of Plate 38) ▷
Whilst it would clearly be unacceptable to pick a rare wildflower and bring it to the drawing board for reference, however complex its structure, we can with an easy conscience put a bunch of curled parsley in a jamjar and study its composition in detail. There can be no substitute for close observation at sketchbook stage in the preparation of your designs and careful pencil shading, with perhaps a suggestion of the directional stitching to follow, can be a great help when embroidery is actually underway (see Fig 36). Remember, too, that a suggestion of shadow in horizontal stitching below a subject can add reality
Dimensions of detail shown:
11.5 x 14cm (4¹/₂ x 5¹/₂in)

◁ *Fig 29*
*Sage (top and in bud) and rosemary (bottom,
with flower) form complicated but pleasing
designs. In the middle distance, as in Plate 38,
their detailed form need only be suggested, but
a knowledge of the anatomy of each plant is
useful if a simplification of its structure is to be
achieved successfully. The rosemary flower
would make an attractive study in detail,
perhaps suitable for mounting into a brooch*

Fig 30 ▽
*Thyme. Rough out a circle to give a format to
the structure. Work the full-faced flowers
first in radial stitching, subsequently
surrounding them with leaves and buds,
working approximately within the parameters
of the sphere. Soften the outline and give a
more natural effect by adding one or two
extra leaves and buds to create an irregular
contour. Finally give the motif support in the
shape of the stem, and so on*

Garden (or common) thyme (*Thymus vulgaris*) is known to have been used by the ancient Egyptians centuries before Christ. The antiseptic and preservative qualities of its essential oil were an integral part of the embalming process. It was subsequently used for flavouring and therapeutic purposes by the Greeks and Romans, and by the seventeenth century in Britain was, according to the astrologer-physician Nicholas Culpeper, a well-known 'women's herb', under the dominion of Venus. Wild thyme shares its many attributes, and has long been regarded as the favourite flower of the fairy kingdom; Oberon in *A Midsummer Night's Dream* describes '...a bank whereon the wild thyme blows'. In the Middle Ages ladies embroidered symbolic favours depicting a bee alighting on a sprig of thyme, which they gave to their suitors (centre and bottom right in Plate 38).

The tiny thyme flowers are arranged in tight whorls around the terminal leaves at the top of the plant's tough, woody stems. To create these charming little spheres, work the flowers first and then intersperse the leaves in short lozenges, or half lozenges, of radial stitching (see Fig 30). Pay particular attention to choosing the correct shades of green – lighter above and darker below – to emphasize the spherical properties of each composite flower-head.

HELEN
STEVENS

A ROSE BY ANY OTHER NAME

I have always used the simple, beautiful flower of the dog rose (*Rosa canina* – Plate 41) to demonstrate the elementary techniques of radial stitching and *opus plumarium* as in Appendix A, page 124. Not only is its open, friendly face a perfect subject, but its uncomplicated loveliness seems to blend well with a thousand other subjects, acting as both backdrop and framework. A chapter concentrating upon plants, therefore, seems a perfect opportunity to explore it and its cultivated relations in their own right.

'Unkempt about those hedges blows, An English unofficial rose…' wrote Rupert Brooke, homesick for Grantchester in the First World War, and indeed, since Tudor times the rose has been a symbol of England – both of her monarchy and the nation herself. However, the rose dates back far beyond British history. Many prehistoric fossils of roses have been found, and the cultivated plant was known in Crete in the sixteenth century BC. The island of Rhodes took its name from the flower. The Romans set great store by roses, constructing hothouses warmed by piped heated water to grow the blooms out of season. They were painted, sculpted and embroidered, and the petals used extravagantly to strew floors and couches, flavour food, scent wine and stuff mattresses – the original 'bed of roses'. In the third century AD, during the reign of Emperor Elagabalus, showers of petals were released through ceiling apertures onto the guests below in such quantities that several suffocated! Such debaucheries so horrified the fathers of the early Christian Church that roses were forbidden inside churches. In later centuries, however, they returned to favour, becoming the emblem of both the Virgin Mary and a host of other saints.

In European folk embroidery, the stylized rose appears in forms which essentially vary little from country to country. They are often seen in profile, changing the usual perspective of the bloom, and in the Middle East this motif was stylized still further to form 'gol', frequently woven into fabrics and carpets. The full-bodied rose is one of the oldest folk-art designs, spanning almost all cultures and periods (Fig 31).

Fig 31 ▽
Across northern and central Europe, folk designs incorporating roses vary little, although the highly stylized format of the flowers becomes less easy to recognize as any particular species (top and middle). In the Middle East the motif was further distorted and 'digitized' to allow for weaving techniques and the 'gol', still supposedly a rose, became a popular motif in Persian and other carpets (bottom)

◁ *PLATE 41*
Rosary beads were originally made from tightly rolled and dried rose petals (hence the name) sweetly perfumed to camouflage unpleasant medieval odours. Simple roses are a symbol of purity – one of the titles of the Virgin Mary is 'The Mystical Rose' – and many other female saints also embrace the rose as their emblem, hence its popular use in stylized ecclesiastical embroidery. Traditionally, the first roses were said to have appeared in Bethlehem when a 'fayre Mayden' was falsely accused and sentenced to death. The faggots of her pyre refused to burn and burst into flower, and by this miracle her innocence was established and she was saved. Roses embroidered into the folk costumes of central and eastern Europe suggested the virginity and purity of the young girls wearing them. The wings of the ladybird (top) are worked in the same straight stitched technique as the bumble bees (see also Plate 38 and Fig 32) 13.5 x 25.5cm (5¼ x 10in)

PLATE 42 ▷

The full-bodied rose, in more recent history, has tended to have rather more voluptuous associations than its single-petalled cousin, having become the archetypal 'lovers bouquet'. As early as the twelfth century cultivated roses could be identified with earthly passions; Fair Rosamund, mistress of Henry II, adopted the name in preference to her own which was much less romantic – simple Jane Clifford. She met her end at the hands of Queen Eleanor who bribed one of Rosamund's ladies to lay a trail to the lady's hidden chamber (for Henry had constructed a labyrinthine house in which to hide her). She did this by stealing Rosamund's embroidery silk and paying it out along the twisting corridors. The queen came to her by this 'clue of thredde and so dealt with her that she lived not long after' wrote a monk of Chester in 1350.

A flower for each season is included in this roundel: rose for summer, crocus for spring, phlox for autumn and aconites for winter. The phlox (Phlox paniculata) and winter aconite (Eranthis) present opposite characteristics, and a pleasing contrast in embroidery. The former appears soft and malleable, the latter rigid and inflexible. This is achieved by working smooth 360 degree radial opus plumarium, voiding lightly between elements. The aconites are worked in sharply angled lozenges of radial work, the voiding emphasized by sharp breaks between fields of embroidery running roughly parallel
20.25cm (8in) round

Fig 32 ▷

In Plates 38 and 41 bumble bees surround the flowers. Their wings are worked as a series of straight, radiating stitches, fanning out to fill the appropriate arc, and leaving a little of the background fabric showing. The ladybird's wings are worked similarly. Transfer only the outline of the wing onto your fabric, and work the radiating stitches to just outside the outline, being careful to follow the line of the curve, as suggested by the diagrams

Despite its simplicity of form, the wild rose should be approached with respect. Careful shadow lining, and an attention to detail when building up the seed-stitched pollen-rich anthers at the core of the bloom, give contrast and emphasis to the rich, glowing directional sweep of stitches which form the broad petals. Opposite angle embroidery, too, is an important element (see Appendix A) to ensure that the saucer-like flowers appear convincingly concave. These rules should also be strictly applied to the foliage, whilst the long, sinuous, cat-clawed stems should curve smoothly; a perfect subject to practise stem stitch. Remember that stem stitch should always be worked *with* the curve of the stem, that is your needle should come up on the *outside* of the curve, returning through the fabric on the line of the transfer (refer to Fig 8, page 24, Chapter One).

The principles learned whilst stitching the simple dog rose can be expanded to cope with the broader scope of directional stitching needed to describe its cultivated, large-flowered relations such as hybrid tea roses and floribundas. A stereotypical bloom is shown in Plate 42 – a single-stemmed frond, terminating in two flower-heads, one fully in bloom, the other still in bud. Deep-centred, multi-petalled flowers can be difficult to render successfully as the core, or growing point, seems to be lost in the complex mass of the petals, and so the correct flow of the directional stitching can be difficult to establish. At the time of preparing your design,

it is helpful to rough out a sketch in which the petals to the front of the subject appear to be transparent, allowing the direction of the stitches on the more distant petals to be pencilled in. When the basic outline is then transferred onto the fabric, you can refer to the 'transparent' sketch to check that your directional stitching falls in the correct direction (see Fig 33). Similarly, the opposite angle stitching for the petals which reflex, curve towards the viewer, or cup away, can be roughed out in advance of stitching, allowing you to concentrate upon colour matching and shading as the work progresses.

The plump bud of the floribunda is essentially very similar in form to the simple bud of the dog rose. The protective sepals which encase the petals reveal their undersides to the viewer, and so should be worked in the appropriate, usually paler, shade of green, contrasting with the shiny, darker upper surfaces of the open sepals supporting the mature flower.

Working on a dark, bold background colour gives a richness to the subject matter, and does not necessitate the use of a shadow line; the voided areas between different fields of embroidery will successfully separate the elements of the design, as in work upon a black background. It means, however, that we must choose the component colours of the design carefully if the overall effect is not to be garish. The peachy, apricot pinks of the rose invite the inclusion of golds and yellows in the shape of aconites and crocuses, whilst the white phlox create a cooling element. A circular framework is provided by the coiling tendril of the bindweed, worked entirely in surface couched gold thread, with only the tiny leaves and buds stitched in silk.

The dancing heads of the crocus (a *chrysanthus* cultivar is shown here), tossed by March winds, is surely one of the most welcome signs of spring. The saffron crocus (*Crocus sativus*) has a long association with the textile industry, as well as being a much-prized drug in the Middle Ages. Gerard commented in his *Herbal* that it '... *maketh the sences more quicke and lively and maketh a man merry*'. Italian ladies, envying the golden locks of their northern sisters, used it to dye their hair blonde, a practice which brought down upon them the wrath of the Church. Henry VIII banned the use of saffron for the dyeing of sheets, as it was reported that ill health resulted from the sheets being too infrequently washed after such applications! The colouring is derived from the dried, crushed stamens of the plant (simply worked on

◁ Fig 33
The growing point or 'core' of the full-bodied
rose (top) is difficult to estimate. Shown as 'X'
on the diagram, the outline of the hidden petals
is suggested by the hatched lines. Seen without
the interference of inner petals, it is easy to infer
the correct direction of the stitches for the large
petal to the right. Even a tiny area such as that
on the left can be extrapolated in the same way
to gauge the correct angle of stitching

◁ *PLATE 43*
*The wide band of rhubarb-red which forms the
largest strata of embroidery on both the upper
and lower wings of the Camberwell beauty*
(Nymphalis antiopa) *demonstrates the
importance of radial stitching to achieve a
variation of shades. It is worked in only one
shade, and yet the play of light on the sweep of
stitches creates the illusion of an infinitely
gradual ranging of colours.*
*The 'gown of green' featured in the Padstow
May Song may well have originally been dyed
with dyer's greenweed, as a specific species of
the plant, low-growing and easy to harvest,
thrives in Cornwall. Many characters in
medieval passion plays and earlier folk rituals
sported elaborate green clothes, from the ancient
'Jack-in-the-Green' embodiment of the
legendary Green Man to later interpretations
of 'the Hooded Man' – Robin Hood*
9.5 x 10.25cm (3¾ x 4in)

the yellow crocus in Plate 42 by small lozenges of straight stitches), requiring 4300 flower-heads to produce one ounce of dye, hence its immense value. The saffron crocus reached England in the reign of Edward II, when a pilgrim returning from Asia Minor secreted several small bulbs in a hollow stave, an act of smuggling for which he would have paid with his life if caught. From these few bulbs the English saffron dyeing industry was established, primarily in the pilgrim's home town of Walden in Essex. The village still bears the name of the plant, which can occasionally be found growing wild in nearby fields.

Another plant boasting a long association with textiles is the dyer's greenweed (*Genista tinctoria*), a small shrubby member of the pea family, related to broom (Plate 43). Initially, like the saffron, it produced a yellow dye, but Flemish immigrants in the fourteenth century developed a process of soaking silk first in the yellow and then plunging it into a vat of blue woad to produce green. The practice spread, and although known as Kendal green after the town in which it was first devised, is probably identical to the well-known Lincoln green, supposedly much beloved of Robin Hood and his Merrie Men! It is a simple, delicate motif for embroidery, the standard, wing and keel petals more easily identifiable than those of the sage and rosemary (Fig 29), and the seed pods which may be straight, curved or coiled are attractive devices. To create the illusion of the seeds within the pods standing proud, work them in stitches which run across the main directional stitching, with a tiny void between the two fields. This method of working separates the elements abruptly, creating the very opposite effect to the smooth dalmatian dog technique used on the blue spots of the Camberwell beauty butterfly. Even the finest of stitching, when laid across the angle of the underlying work, immediately becomes noticeable, as demonstrated here on the upper edges of the butterfly's wing, where an extremely narrow black silk thread has been whipped over the yellow border to create lifelike, detailed markings.

CORN DOLLIES

The spring ritual of the Lady's wain, with its embroidered covering, pulled from field to field to ensure good fortune and fruitfulness for the coming summer, had its autumn counterpart in the veneration of the Lady, or Goddess, as Harvest Queen.

Traditionally, an effigy would be made, fashioned from the whole last corn stook, adorned richly in the same manner as the mystical wain, to embody the spirit of the harvest. It would be carefully preserved throughout the winter, and in early

PLATE 44 ▷
More often associated with spring, the chirpy butterball antics of young chicks can be a delight in the farmyard at almost any time of the year. Here, the soft, fluffy texture of their down is achieved by working short straight stitches, fairly widely spaced, following the contours of their rounded bodies. Shadow lining is broken and worked in the same direction as the overall sweep of stitches, and a three-dimensional effect described by working shades of grey into the yellow on the undersides. The matt, eggshell finish on the broken egg is created by a single strand of stranded cotton, with darker brown markings incorporated by the use of dalmatian dog technique
14 x 13.5cm (5½ x 5¼in)

◁ *PLATE 45*
Originally worked as a demonstration piece,
this goldwork has been mounted on an oval
backing, and fitted with a brooch pin. It makes
a rich, spectacular addition to an autumn
outfit; the contrasting textures of brown velvet
and glowing gold thread never fail to attract
comment. Be adventurous with your work –
even samples and experimental snippets can be
converted into tiny masterpieces!
Overall height: 8cm (3¼in)

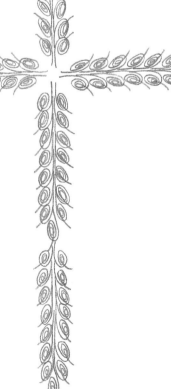

spring laid in a grave cut by the first furrow of the plough, to be resurrected in the guise of the new season's growth. Gleaning was an important boon for the poor, and in some communities a mortal embodiment of the Harvest Queen was set in charge of the women undertaking this task. She wielded the power to regulate the beginning and end of work and often the costumes of these ritualistic principal players received considerable attention. The Padstow May Song reflects an equivalent attention to such details: 'Arise up, all in your gown of green, you are as fine a lady as wait upon the Queen... Arise up, all in your cloak of silk...'

  ' The Lady's effigy gradually dwindled to the smaller 'corn dollies' of more recent centuries, still popular today, occasionally decorated with ribbons and embroidered scraps, and the continuing potency of grain as a symbol and staple of life is understandably pan-cultural. The many references to cereal crops in the Bible makes corn, barley and other grains popular subjects for church embroideries, and a lifelike study of wheat, such as that included in Plate 44, can be adapted into a pleasing goldwork motif (Plate 45), which could be repeated at regular intervals to decorate a large expanse of fabric, or arranged geometrically to effect more complicated figures (Fig 34).

    The whiskers of the wheat-ear are shorter than those of many other grains (oats or barley, for instance) and so even if rendered in naturalistic form could be left

Fig 34 ▷
The goldwork motif in Plate 44 could be used in
many ways to create attractive church embroideries.
Here, the basic element has been arranged to create
a cross, suitable for a lectern or pulpit fall

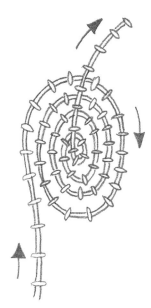

◁ *Fig 35*
Work each grain of the ear separately, from the bottom upwards, in the direction shown. Couch the threads evenly, allowing the stitches to become closer together as the spiral decreases towards the centre of the motif. As the 'whisker' is taken across the rest of the design, try to work the couching stitches between the already worked coil of goldwork, anchoring it firmly at the far tip

Fig 36 △

Cornflowers. Embroider the main petals first, shadow lining as indicated if working on a pale background (top). Soften the outline by adding the tips of the petals to the back of the head, and the tiny lozenges of radial stitches to create the 'pincushion' at the centre of the flower. Superimpose seed stitches to suggest the dancing anthers on their invisible stamens. The leaves of the curled parsley (bottom and Plate 38) are worked similarly, without the complication of the central elements

as single straight stitches upon the background fabric. When stylized, as in Plate 45, their length can be adapted to suit the needs of the chosen design. Here the motif is worked upon brown velvet, which allows the surface couched gold thread to nestle snugly into the pile of the fabric; an advantage when using genuine gold thread, which cannot be taken through the fabric for finishing on the reverse. Begin each coiled grain at the stem of the motif, anchoring the gold firmly with a second couching stitch at the very tip of the thread. Work the gold in a decreasing, oval coil towards the centre of the grain, and then take the 'whisker' across the outer top quadrant of the coil, allowing it to extend as far as desired before cutting the gold thread, and again whipping it down firmly at the very tip. This order of stitching is set out in Fig 35.

The pretty blue cornflower (*Centaurea cyanus*) was once a common weed of arable fields, and though like the poppy an irritation to farmers, its passing can hardly fail to be mourned. A bright haze of blue shimmering in the fields now is more likely to be a carefully managed crop of flax than the haphazard dotting of 'blue bonnets', as the cornflower was locally known. The complicated flower-head can be approached similarly to the curly parsley described on page 67. Light and dark shades of blue differentiate between outer and inner sides of each small inflorescence, whilst the 'pincushion' at the centre of the flower-head is worked in tiny lozenges of radial stitching (see Fig 36). Scaly, protective sepals cup the unopened bud, carefully shadow lined.

Despite our nostalgic longing for the apparently idyllic scenes of long-lost rural life, there is still tremendous charm to be found in the modern countryside, and where once the harvest was cut by hand, and then by horse-drawn machine, the droning whirr of a distant combine harvester, like a huge mythological beast as it cuts its magnificent swathe through the crops, is now the very essence of late summer. Why pretend that it isn't there? The study in Plate 46, commissioned as a gift for a member of a farming family, shows the modern countryside at its best.

Treating the machine impressionistically alleviates the need to study the

technical side of its composition too deeply. Its essential solidity and power is needed, and this is achieved by firm shadow lining and sharp, angular stitching, which is echoed in the cut crop, lying in alternating rows in the background. Clothing the driver (a mere suggestion of the human form) in the same bright red as the foreground poppy ensures that the eye is drawn to him, putting that distant character at the core of the picture. Upright straight stitches, worked in horizontal ranks, increasing in size towards the front of the study, overlap each other slightly, giving density to the crop, and on the far skyline the trees throw shadows onto the sunny incline. The old song of the Harvest Home is still appropriate:

> *Master's got his corn,*
> *Well mawn, well shorn,*
> *Ne'er heeled over, ne'er stuck fast,*
> *Harvest has come home at last.*

PLATE 46 △

My farming friends claim the manufacture of this combine harvester is given away by its colour – yellow means Claas! I have to confess that the shade was chosen for its overall suitability to the scene. Impressive and attractive (to some) as such a machine may be, too bright a shade would dominate the more natural colours of the study; the yellow is distinctive and yet not overpowering
12.75 x 14cm (5 x 5½in)

. . . .

CHAPTER FIVE

QUESTS, JOURNEYS AND BATTLES

The Boar images shone over the cheek armour,
decked with gold…
Beowulf spoke – on him his corslet shone,
The shirt of mail sewn by the hand of the Smith –
'Send to Hygelac, if battle takes me off
the best of battle garments that arm my breast'

Beowulf
Germanic-origin epic, c. Sixth Century

 TILL the fire burned, but less brightly, an occasional leaping flame teasing the tapestry figures to life. The Story-teller gathered his patterned cloak around him more closely as he spoke:

'Womens' art or no, needle and thread, warp and weft, have played their part in men's battles and quests. I recall the tale of Sigurd, the mighty hero who slew the dragon Fadmir and reclaimed the fabled treasure of the Rhinegold. After pledging his love to Brynhild, he was tricked by a witch's cunning into marrying Gudrun. Wearing a magically woven cloak he slept a night by his own true love's side, taking the appearance of her husband-to-be, Gunnar. Brynhild and Gudrun were friends, often working together on their embroideries. When each boasted to the other in stitches of her husband's prowess the deceptions came to light. Brynhild ripped the embroidered tales of Sigurd's deeds to shreds, and demanded her honour be avenged. Sigurd was slain, and Brynhild, overcome by grief, killed herself to be beside him for ever in the tapestry-decked halls of Valhalla.'

PLATE 48 △

'S' By the thirteenth century, illuminated manuscripts were becoming increasingly ethereal. Literary ideals were of courtly love, troubadours and romantic prose, and in 1485 Caxton printed the first version of Le Morte D'Arthur. *A typical tracery of foliage and blossom is finely worked in silk on a vibrant background, an impression of fluttering petals given by random seed beads. A consistent theme of colour has been used for the three birds – from the top: swallow, redstart and nuthatch – which were sketched and subsequently embroidered in the style of a French manuscript. Two strands of very fine silk have been used throughout*
9.5 x 13.25cm (3¾ x 5¼in)

KNIGHT ERRANT

Chivalry, fortitude and bravery: the three essential characteristics of the true hero, whether he be rescuing damsels in distress, reaching for the impossible dream or facing a deadly foe. Long before the written word these concepts crystallized to shape the folklore, fables and fairy tales of northern Europe and when they were eventually recorded brought with them an echo of the distant worlds in which they were formed – an echo in the epic poetry recounting fantastic deeds and a reflection in unexpectedly vivid descriptions of fantastic furnishings, fine clothing, love tokens and magic rituals.

The unknown writer of *Beowulf*, the sixth-century Anglo-Saxon poem, describes the mighty hall of Heorot where '…woven hangings gleamed, gold adorned, on the walls' and in the *Mabinogion*, a Celtic masterpiece of uncertain date (though certainly prior to the tenth century) King Arthur sits 'with a coverlet of yellow-red brocaded silk' while Gwenhwyfar (Guinevere) and her handmaidens are sewing at a window. In *Sir Gawain* a love token is an embroidered girdle; in the *Volsungasaga* (later immortalized by Wagner in the Ring Cycle) magic swords are forged by plaiting threads of molten iron – the textile imagery is endless. As late as the nineteenth century Tennyson continues the tradition in the *Idylls of the King*, describing the Lady of the Lake as 'clothed in white samite, mystic, wonderful'. The overtly male figure of the hero is always surrounded by the female arts, and it was apparently important for that fact to be emphasized. How can we capture that spirit of mystery and adventure?

Many of the early sagas contain more than a shred of real history. Beowulf was of the race of the Geats, a tribe in what is now southern Sweden, and his 'hearth companion', Hygelac, was a historical character. Descriptions of the Great Hall, the tapestries and the boar-crested armour have been proved accurate by archaeology. It takes only a short leap of the imagination for us to enter that world of epic battles and story-telling. In Plate 47 my protagonists take animal form. This was a scene which I actually witnessed between a domesticated wild boar piglet and a magnificent cockerel. The imagery seemed obvious: the boar always a symbol of bravery (hence the boar crests) and the cockerel a cipher for pride. The scene has been treated entirely naturalistically, with the magnificent cockerel bristling with fury at the jaunty interference of the tiny piglet. Eye-to-eye contact has been established by highlighting the correct eye alignment, and a contrast in the texture of feathers and rough hide created by the respective use of floss silk and stranded cotton. An 'epic' location for the encounter is suggested by the feeling of home, created by the piglet's sow and siblings to one side of the scene, and by drawing the eye to the distant horizon via the meandering pathway, scrub and ultimately the converging hills; these devices were used throughout medieval art to convey symbolic or mythological landscapes. Whilst such naturalistic elements would not have been a feature of the 'gold adorned' hangings of Heorot, the symbolism would certainly have been appreciated. After his battle with the monster Grendel, Beowulf was rewarded with many treasures, including a great stitched banner emblazoned with a boar emblem.

◁ *PLATE 47 (page 80 – 81)*

A showdown at noon! The wild boar (Sus scrofa) is the ancestor of all domestic pigs and the only wild member of the pig family to be found in Europe. Extinct in Britain in the wild since the seventeenth century, it is now enjoying something of a renaissance both as a farmed animal and an exhibition 'rare breed'. When born, and for several months, the piglets are deeply camouflaged with stripes and spots, echoing their natural woodland habitat. They are aggressively inquisitive – the nose-down, tail-up stance shown here is typical.

Just as birds have a 'jizz' – an archetypal stance and way of moving – so many other animals are immediately recognizable by their attitude. Try to capture it in your work. Whilst reference books are essential for accurate markings, environments, and the like, there is no substitute for personal observation. Rough notes and sketches are invaluable later at the drawing board. If you feel that an original sketch is beyond you, working from a photograph is fine – but remember that you are working an embroidery of a pig, not an embroidery of a photograph of a pig! What works in one medium will not necessarily work in another

Embroidery shown life-size:
40.5 x 28cm (16 x 11in)

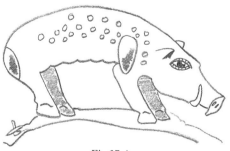

Fig 37 △

Boar crests, as mentioned in Beowulf, *were thought to offer protection to the wearer. This splendid bronze crest, dating from the seventh century, is from the Benty Grange helmet (now in Sheffield City Museum)*

PLATE 49 ▷

The Norse god Freyr was a gentle god of peace and plenty. He rode the boar Gullinbursti, who was also his protector and symbol. Followers celebrated Freyr's festival at Yuletide, when a boar was sacrificed. The serving of a boar's head at Christmas was a derivation of this ritual, as is the inclusion of pork among the traditional meats of the festive season to this day.

Saxon jewellers and embroiderers were fascinated by colour and sparkle, and used a wide variety of semi-precious stones in their work. It is now possible to buy small, roughly cut or uncut stones, ready drilled with tiny holes and suitable for application to the finest of work. Don't be afraid to be adventurous – in a stylized piece of work, the addition of another dimension in the shape of beads or stones can be a real revelation

11.5 x 7.25cm (4½ x 3in)

PLATE 50 ▷

A combination of fibres have been used here to create a variety of effects and 'depths' within the scene as a whole. The goldwork of the lettering and ribbon interlace, which creates a frame for the 'action' within, is conventional and static, as is the sun/crucifix motif. The figure and the horse are worked naturalistically in silk and wool; here there is movement, suggested by the breeze tugging the horse's tail and the flick of the mane as it tosses its head. As the scene recedes we again enter a realm of stylized motifs: the tree, the sharply defined colours of the landscape, the suggestion of sky framing the cross. As in all good fairy tales the main character is in a slightly alien environment. Brithnoth's story may be true, but it has all the elements of a good adventure yarn

29.25 x 31.75cm (11½ x 12½in)

Possibly a closer approximation to the style of the banner would be an adaptation of the Viking-inspired boar clasp found at the Sutton Hoo ship burial in Suffolk, dating from the seventh century (Plate 49).

In Chapter One (Plate 17) we explored the translation of relief-carved stonework into embroidery. Here we turn to the exuberant design of Anglo-Saxon metalwork for our inspiration. Originally one of a pair, the boar motif is composed of a pair of interlocking animals. Red, blue and black silk take the place of garnets and *millefiori* glass, a suggestion of earth and sky created by goldstone chips and blue quartz. Red silk is worked in various directions to create a variety of hues, each field separated from the next by infilling the voids with surface couched gold passing thread. On the front half of each figure the silk has been overlaid in the same shade to subtly alter the texture, and on the front haunches blue and black silk is needle woven in a broad laddering stitch to give a chequerboard effect. Boar motifs represented strength, bravery and a tenacious spirit; the Celts believed that the boar was so formidable a foe that they adopted it as a symbol of war, and the Celtic battle horn, the tarnik, had a mouth in the shape of a baying boar's head (see Fig 37).

Long before the Crusades the concept of 'holy war', the righteous taking up of arms to defend home and hearth, gave rise to many heroic figures, some legendary, some authentically historic, which inspired the people and attracted a whole body of folklore and fable over the centuries. The Celtic Cuchulainn who single-handedly withstood the forces of Queen Medb (usually depicted with a fabulous woven cloak); Boudicca's resistance against the Romans; King Arthur's ('last of the Romans') fight against the incursion of the Saxons: each civilization in turn had its resistance leader and, ultimately hopeless, cause. At the close of the tenth century the Saxons were faced by the Danish invasion, and a hero emerged whose exploits were told in an epic embroidery once as famous as the Bayeux Tapestry.

Brithnoth was ealdorman of Essex when a huge fleet of Danish ships, lead by Olaf Trygvasson, threatened to invade the East Anglian coast. In an epic ride

throughout the eastern shires of England he rallied an enormous force of fighting men, returning to the Blackwater estuary just in time to engage the enemy. He might have held them off but for a chivalrous act in which he allowed the Danish army to pass over the causeway from their island campsite onto the mainland to do battle. Overwhelmed by their numbers he, and his whole army, fell. During his lifetime he had been a patron of Ely Abbey in Cambridgeshire and his body was taken there after the battle. Aelfflaed, his wife, was a skilled needlewoman and with her ladies worked a vast narrative embroidery which for many years hung in the abbey. Some 100 years later when Bishop Odo, half-brother to William the Conqueror, saw the hanging, he so admired the concept that he ordered a similar piece to be worked depicting his brother's invasion of England – and so the Bayeux Tapestry was born.

Brithnoth was one of a long line of Saxon heroes – later including Hereward the Wake and Robin Hood – but he has always been my personal favourite. Plate 50 is my tribute to him, and to his wife's long-lost embroidery. Combining a stylized format with less formal elements, he is seen in the rolling Essex countryside, sword drawn, basking in a sun which doubles as a symbol of Christianity; his foes were pagan. Bold use of shadowing effects has been used here to create a sharp, lucid

Fig 38 △
The split stitch used to describe the face and hands of figures in medieval embroidery was worked rather idiosyncratically, always in spirals inward towards the cheeks, chin and centre of the forehead, but as the figure itself is stylized this presents no real artistic anomaly.

For a contemporary interpretation of the human figure (Plate 50) the split stitch follows the natural contours of the face and features

Fig 39 ▷
Being imaginative in the interpretation of various elements of a landscape is hardly innovative! Whilst using rosettes to suggest the foliage of the tree in Plate 50 is startling (left), it can hardly compare with the amazing arboreal creations in the Bayeux Tapestry (right). Though nearing the end of its high-fashion status towards the close of the tenth century, interlace design still wielded a powerful fascination

◁ *PLATE 51 (detail of Plate 50)*
The zoomorphic beasts used here are inspired by
manuscripts of the seventh and eighth
centuries. As a patron of the church, Brithnoth
would have been familiar with such books – it
is recorded that he was an educated man – and
Aelfflaed might well have used similar designs
in her own work. She and the female members
of her family gave many fine embroideries to
Ely and other abbeys, and Aelswith,
Brithnoth's grand-daughter, established a
thriving community of embroiderers in the
Cambridgeshire fens. Abbey documentation
records many of the pieces which they produced,
fine ecclesiastic embroideries from the very
dawning of Opus Anglicanum
6.5 x 9cm (2½ x 3½in)

quality, as if looking through a window into another dimension; rather than working the tree in fine, seed-stitched foliage, rosettes of greenery are used to emphasize light and dark areas and vivid contrasts of shade in the background continue the theme. Combining and contrasting with these starkly modern effects, the ancient technique of split stitch has been used on the face and hands (just as it would during the tenth century) and broad areas have been covered with surface couched gold and silver. A study such as this necessitates a certain amount of historical research; for example, it would be foolish to show a medieval hero with a modern saddle and bridle. Like the Western cowboys of the nineteenth century, a fighting man needed to be comfortable and secure on his horse; here the effect of sheepskin has been created by using undyed wool worked in chunky seed stitches, darkened near the pommel and girth by interspersing grey stranded cotton.

A particularly elaborate illumination (Plate 51) has been effected on the initial 'B' of Brithnoth's name as it was spelled in Anglo-Saxon – Byrhtnod – the terminal

'd' is actually the Saxon letter pronounced 'th'. A fine gauge of gold passing thread has been surface couched to create the body of the letter, and the zoomorphic head and feet and interlaced smaller animal worked in silk to imitate the flux of enamel in jewellery of the period. The inclusion of a highlight in the eye brings even such highly stylized creatures to life.

LIVING LEGENDS

According to Arthurian legend, the search for the Holy Grail was the quest which obsessed the Knights of the Round Table above all others. It could only be attained by one whose purity surpassed all others and, once found, had the power to cure all ills, restore all that was lost and maintain the realm in perpetual freedom. Tradition held that it had been brought to Avalon from the Holy Land and hidden to be found at the time of greatest need but even Lancelot, the bravest of all Arthur's knights, could only glimpse it 'on a table of silver covered with red samite' according to Malory's *Le Morte D'Arthur*, and even there, the holy of holies is protected by a fine decorated textile. Ultimately Camelot fell, taking with it any clues as to the Grail's ultimate resting place.

The Grail can be very much a personal concept. In Plate 52 I have chosen to represent it as a fragile thing of beauty, camouflaged by, and in turn protecting, the natural world. Working on a black background I wanted to achieve a suggestion of water and glass, semi-transparent, but with clean, strong lines. This has been effected by using a delicate rainbow-shaded blending filament and clear sequins, contrasting with entirely accurate colours to describe the natural elements of the design.

It is difficult to judge the overall effect of the finished piece in sketch form, and so the outline of the chalice can be roughed out initially on the background fabric in white pencil, the decorative elements laid loosely in place. At this experimental stage you can be as innovative as you choose; for a bolder effect beads, shisha glass or coloured sequins could be used. Once you are satisfied with the design make a note of the arrangement of the decoration and copy the outline of the vessel onto your tracing paper, adding the butterflies or other naturalistic elements. Reposition the sketch as accurately as possible over the white pencilled outline on your fabric and transfer the butterflies and so on in the usual way. Embroider these elements first. Block in any solid areas of the chalice in

◁ PLATE 52

The Butterfly Grail. One of the Grail legends suggests that the vessel was in the keeping of the Knights Templar, the crusading order of knights both feared and revered throughout the Middle Ages. During the Crusades, St John's-wort was used to heal the wounded: according to the 'doctrine of signatures' which stipulated that a plant could heal any ill in any part of the body which it resembled, the many tiny holes (actually translucent glands) in its leaves represented sword and spear punctures. It should therefore be capable of curing wounds, especially those received in battle. Common St John's-wort (Hypericum perforatum) was also valued for its power to drive away demons and evil spirits, and its perforated leaves were said to be the result of the devil's attack upon the plant with St Dunstan's embroidery needle! (see The Embroiderer's Countryside*).*

The star-shaped flowers and oval leaves are simply worked in embroidery; only the central pompons of stamens and anthers need special attention. Work the petals first, then a starburst of fine straight lines in red to create the cluster of stamens. Scatter seed stitches in yellow at the top of the starburst, overlaying the petals in places to create a natural effect (see order of working in Fig 40)
13.25 x 19cm (5¼ x 7½in)

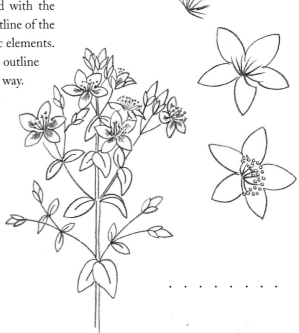

Fig 40 ▷
St John's-wort forms a design full of angles and triangles. Its geometric character is softened somewhat by the pretty flowers, their petals simply worked in directional stitching, softened by the orange-red powder puffs at the centre of each

· · · · · · · ·

PLATE 53 ▷
Unicorns and the Holy Grail have an affinity in
legend. One of the guardians of the
Grail is Beate:

…living by the lot of mortals: to love, to suffer
Without knowledge, yet mindful of her home
And the Unicorn, and pure service
Chaste as none…

Parzival, *Albrecht von Schaeffer, 1922*

10.25 (4in) round including frame

Fig 41 △
A landscape miniature such as Plate 53
uses the arching tree to echo the curve of the
frame. In a close-up study, similarly framed, a
sinuous plant such as convolvulus could do
the same job, leaving the lower area open for
the inclusion of your chosen subject. (It could
even be used to frame an even tinier
landscape.) This idea has been used in a larger
format in Plate 42, page 73

satin stitch, and to create a smooth outline surface couch the blending filament to form the cup and base. Separate out the cellophane strand from the filament and use this to stitch the sequins in place – in this way no opaque stitches will interfere with the wholly transparent effect. If a sequin 'disappears' behind a solid element of the design cut it cleanly and stitch it into place at the correct angle (as in the case of the large sequin abutting the upper wing of the peacock butterfly). Add any other beads or mirrors to complete the study.

Take particular care in the presentation of a piece such as this. Iron the reverse of the work on a cool setting (see Appendix B), at no time allowing the iron into direct contact with the cellophane filament. Mount the embroidery in the usual way and pay particular attention to removing every trace of loose silk or lint; even a speck will detract from the ethereal effect. Use a window mount to keep the glass well away from the raised elements when framing.

The choice of presentation can be extremely important in a fantasy study, and fussy framing often detracts from the subject matter. In Plate 53 the effect is of a magical microcosm – rather like the tiny enclosed world of a paperweight snowstorm – the simple silver frame holding its contents apart from the real world, yet drawing the eye to its most important features, the silver horns of the unicorns.

Creatures of myth and mystery since time immemorial, unicorns have often appeared in embroidery and tapestry, most famously in the 'Lady and Unicorn' and 'Hunt of the Unicorn' series of tapestries, worked in the fifteenth century (either of Flemish or French origin). Legend holds that the unicorn can only be tamed by a virgin, in whose lap it will trustingly lay its head. This connection with virginity gave rise to the creature's symbolic value to the medieval Christian in the romantic realms of beauty, lost innocence and a world without sin. That the unicorn truly existed was never doubted – the narwhal's horns which appeared throughout the Middle Ages in Europe (the narwhal then being an entirely unknown species) were cited as proof enough.

An elegant white horse with a silver horn and a goat's beard, the unicorn (and its foal) make charming subjects. Treated simply, in white and two shades of grey, together with the essential shadow line, they make a delightful miniature study. Use the curve of the frame to give overall cohesion to the supporting elements of the design, allowing the branches of the tree to arch across the motif and lead the eye to the distant horizon. Even in a small embroidery it is possible to include a successful suggestion of distance and perspective by alternating light and dark shades, and matt and floss textures, to capture the impression of passing sunlight and shadow on the distant hills.

Fig 42 △
An oval miniature frame could use iris or other tall plants to curve inwards, focusing the eye upon the main element – a tiny dragonfly would make this an exquisite design

THE EMPEROR'S NEW CLOTHES

Tussah, samite, seda floja – silk's pseudonyms trip off the tongue like a magical incantation. No other fibre has such a fabulous pedigree or well-deserved reputation for beauty and strength. Yet silk is produced by a strange little moth, the *Bombyx mori*, which after centuries of captivity cannot fly and can only walk short distances on its favoured food plant, the white mulberry (*Morus alba*). Far Eastern legend asserts that long ago there lived an emperor's favourite daughter, a princess whose hair was like golden thread. Her stepmother hated her because of her great beauty, and five times tried to kill her, but on each occasion the princess fell asleep and was rescued. Finally the stepmother hollowed out the trunk of a mulberry tree and shut the princess inside, tossing the trunk into the sea. It was washed up onto the coast of Japan and, when opened, its beautiful captive opened her eyes and immediately changed into a silkworm. Eventually the silkworm wrapped itself in a cocoon of golden threads, later emerging as a shimmering white moth; and so the practice of sericulture (silk production) began in Japan.

Plate 54 shows silk moths on white mulberry. The stubby body and small wings of the moth are entirely white, broken only by segmentation and veining in black; head, thorax and abdomen are all covered with a soft, downy hair, complemented by magnificent feathered antennae. This, together with their large black eyes, gives silk moths the appearance of rather affable, moustached old gentlemen. The heads and bodies should be worked in ranks of split stitch, with voids left between the segments, then softened by feathering over with short straight stitches. Needle weave a short laddered line of black silk between each segment and, using the same thread, work a line of ticking in the same direction as the underlying stitches to differentiate between head and body. Highlight the satin-stitched eye with white

Fig 43 ▽

Short, sharp stitching in various directions creates the individual fruits of the compound mulberry, tiny seed stitches suggesting the tip of each. These curtailed stitches make a superb contrast with the broad sweeps of directional stitches on the leaves. Pay particular attention to the directional sweep if these are to be fully successful

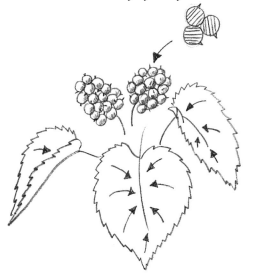

PLATE 54 ▷

According to legend, silk moths first came to Europe hidden in the hollow centre of a bamboo cane, smuggled out of China by an old Italian monk. This tale is strangely similar to the supposed arrival of saffron in England, as mentioned in Chapter Four.

The pure white moths, worked against a pale background, would be insignificant. Here they are mainly juxtaposed on the bright-green mulberry leaves, and an apricot background fabric has been chosen to give relief where they overlap. Distinctive colours can be effective as a base for natural history subjects (see also Plate 55), but care should be taken that they do not overwhelm the main subject. Before transferring your design lay out your coloured silks on the proposed background fabric and ensure that they neither clash nor subdue each other

13 x 13cm (5 x 5in)

and work the antennae in a fine line of stem stitch, softened by straight stitches to create the feathery effect. The wings are worked simply in long radial stitches, lightly woven through with three rows of laddering.

Mulberry is a delightful motif and is a tree steeped in legend. It was often included in samplers designed in the seventeenth century when James I encouraged the planting of mulberries in an attempt to rear silkworms for the home production of silk. However, the king had been badly advised, and having been party to the planting of hundreds of black mulberry trees found that silkworms required the white variety, which does not grow well in northern Europe. The result was no silk industry, but many beautiful mulberry trees, many of which still survive today.

Wrongly identifying black and white mulberries must have been an easy mistake to make, for the two species are very similar. Plate 54 shows the white mulberry. The fruits range from fleshy white to pink (rather than the deep wine-red of the black mulberry) and give us a good opportunity to practise working composite fruit-heads. The colours are graduated from light to dark, beginning with the lowest

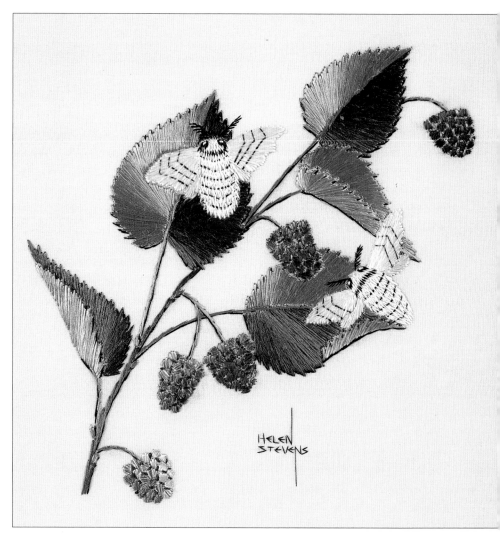

◁ *PLATE 55*
'... with a shillelagh under my arm, and a
twinkle in my eye' many an Irishman set off on
a journey – for the traditional Irish cudgel, the
shillelagh, is made of blackthorn wood, used on
account of its toughness and its ability to ward
off the 'little people'. It is tempting to work long
straight elements of a design in slanting stitches
– such as the sinuous snake stitches used for
curving, reflexing shapes – but to create an
impression of strength, the stitches must run
with the grain of the wood depicted, along the
length of the branch or stem. This gives a rigid,
firm line to the finished work (see Fig 44)
7.75 x 14cm (3 x 5½in)

fruit, which would be the last to ripen. Work each individual segment of the fruit separately, in a slightly different direction to its neighbours, and intersperse tiny seed stitches to suggest the withered tips which once supported the catkin flowers (see Fig 43). The broad swathes of directional *opus plumarium* describing each side of the shiny, heart-shaped leaves make a pleasing contrast with the closely worked berries.

The only native British member of the silk moth family is the impressive emperor moth (Plate 55 – see also Plate 19). In July and August its caterpillars make tough, egg-shaped cocoons, which over-winter to hatch the following May. Unfortunately the silk produced is not strong enough to spin. Often attracted to heather, the emperor will lay its eggs on any of its food plants, which include bramble, loosestrife, elder and (shown here) sloe.

· · · · · · · ·

PLATE 56 ▷

*The oxalis is a native of South Africa and
thrives in warm conditions. In Devon
and Cornwall it is a garden escapee and has
become naturalized in woodlands, hedge
banks and stone walls, where it is a lovely sight
from late spring to midsummer. In the absence
of its flowers it can be mistaken for clover.
There can be no confusing the glorious purple
emperor though with any other butterfly – if
you are lucky enough to see one. Rare now, it
occurs only in certain protected woodland
locations, where once it skimmed the treetops in
hundreds. We can enjoy its beauty through the
medium of shimmering silk without disturbing
its natural habitat.*

*Purple is one of the most difficult colours to
photograph successfully. Do not always trust
photographic handbooks when colour matching
your silks; if you want to be accurate use a
painted illustration as your source*
11 x 18cm (4½ x 7in)

The strong pattern of the emperor moth's wings is picked out in subtly blending shades. Apart from the startling blue upper edges and tips to the wings, the female (who is the larger of the two) is almost entirely cream and grey, but the juxtaposition of the colours make a magnificent show. As with the Kentish glory (Plate 32) approach the design step-by-step, remembering the principles of dalmatian dog technique and radial stitching: the distinctive false eyes should be worked first, then the variously coloured strata built up from the inside of the motif (the insect's body) outwards. A similar order of working should be adopted for the smaller male. The body and antennae should be worked in the usual way.

Sloe bushes, more commonly called blackthorn (*Prunus spinosa*) are, as their Latin name suggests, fiercely spiny. They have been used as protective barriers since medieval times, and it is a very brave prince who hacks his way through those vicious thorns to his Sleeping Beauty's castle. Acutely angled chevron stitching illustrates them well. Work in a fairly broad gauge of thread – these are serious prickles – remembering to use a lighter shade on the upper edge of the composite stitch. A pleasing contrast is effected between this sharp, angular motif and the perfectly round sloes.

It is, perhaps, not surprizing that the most magnificent members of various species are quite often called 'emperors'. The emperor dragonfly, emperor moth and purple emperor butterfly are all among the most beautiful of their kinds. In Plate 56 I have used the purple emperor (*Apatura iris*) to create a picture which perfectly illustrates the glories of sleave (fine untwisted, or floss) silk. The motifs are simple: the oxalis leaves and flowers are uninterrupted strata and bands of radial work and the butterfly, basking in the beauty of its superb colour, has minimal markings. In the nineteenth century the entomologist Edward Newman compared the iridescent colours of the male purple emperor to Roman 'robes of Tyrian purple' and, indeed, the butterfly's name also harks back to the Classics – Iris was the Greek messenger of the gods who spoke through the rainbow. All this and more can be captured in silk, its glowing properties unencumbered by complicated stitching.

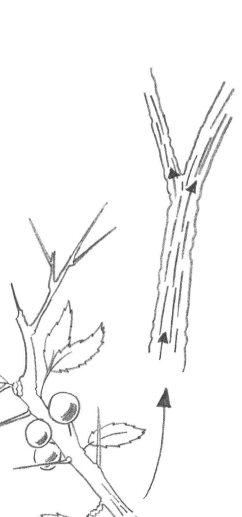

Fig 44 ▷

Hardwood should appear rigid rather than sinuous, so work the stitches along the grain of the branch, allowing straight stitches to blend together in a linear, rather than radial, pattern

CHAPTER SIX

ANIMAL MAGIC

Said the Cat,
'take a strand of the thread you are spinning
and tie it to your spinning-whorl
and drag it along the floor;
and I will show you a Magic…'

The Cat That Walked Alone
Rudyard Kipling (1902)

HELEN
STEVENS

WITH a sudden scurry, a mouse scampered across the floor. Both my Lady and the Story-teller jumped, startled, and then my Lady laughed:

'Come, come, our tales have become much too sad and solemn for such a dark night – do you know how the tabby cat got her markings? It is said that long ago in the East a poor maiden had a baby. She and her husband were away from home when the baby was born, they had to seek shelter where they could, and the baby had no toys. When he cried, she could not hush him. The soft cooing of the doves did not help, nor did the warm milk of the cow, nor the comforting presence of the brown-eyed donkey. The maiden sat at her sewing, but could not work for the cries of the baby, when a cat sprang in the window and began to pat at the embroidery thread. The cat jumped at the thread, rolled head over heels, pretended to lose it, found it, chased it between her hind paws, pounced again and again until the baby chuckled as loudly as he had cried. Then she curled up in the baby's arms and sang him to sleep. Blessing the cat for her cleverness, the maiden took the thread and arranged it in a pretty pattern on the cat's grey fur – and the markings have been there ever since. Especially on the tabby's forehead, where it makes a mark like the letter 'M'. For some people say that the maiden's name was Mary.'

PLATE 58 △

'W' The idea of combining the stylized with the entirely naturalistic has been used again here. The mouse and the blackberries have been rendered faithfully, down to the last quiver of the mouse's whiskers as it reaches for the juiciest berry, but both its tail and the stem of the bramble frond have been intertwined with the 'W' to echo the interlace of the letter's design. However, in order to ensure that the diversity of subject matter is not too stark, deep and pale green, outlined in gold, have been chosen for the letter, following the woodland theme. The body of the mouse has been worked with attention to the same details as the cat in Plate 57. The ratio of scale mouse:cat is approximately true to life, but proportionately the 'feathering' between voids and the length of the directional stitches themselves are smaller, to allow for the appropriate details to be included in the smaller animal. The blackberries are worked similarly to the mulberries in Plate 54, page 92

9.5 x 13.25cm (3³/₄ x 5¹/₄in)

THE OWL AND THE PUSSYCAT

Anyone who has ever had a pet will be aware of the magic that an animal can spin. It weaves itself around your heart and becomes an integral part of your life until it is impossible to imagine the pattern of your existence without it. Throughout mankind's evolution this has been more than an emotional tie; man's best friend was just that when life or death depended upon the success of the day's hunt, when a horse was your sole means of transport or an ox the only way of tilling your land. They provided food, clothing, protection and, later, companionship. Small wonder that animals both tame and wild became totems, the physical embodiment of the gods, or even gods themselves.

Perhaps the most familiar animal which today we associate with lost civilizations is the cat and its veneration in ancient Egypt. Because it was hostile to rats and snakes it became a sacred animal, first in the shape of the wild jungle cat which lived in the thickets of the Nile delta, and later as the domestic cat. The 'great cat who dwells in Heliopolis' was sacred to the sun — and to watch a cat bask in the sunshine is to understand the imagery! Plate 57 was inspired by my own cat, a sturdy English tabby-and-white, at rest beneath the inverted 'V', a pyramid formed by the legs of a deckchair. Symbolic motifs (clockwise from the left) are the sacred eye of Horus, the ankh, the scarab beetle and the winged disk, all designs which feature widely in the architecture and ceramics of ancient Egypt.

Plate 57 is worked on pure slub silk, chosen for its colour and texture to imitate the qualities of sand and desert. The pyramids and the skyline beyond are mere suggestions, worked in a couched line of 2/1T black and gold thread, allowing full attention to be given to the main features without the interference of a complex background. The symbols are worked in satin stitch and couching, bold, simple fields of single colours which allow immediate recognition, even at a distance. The intricacies of directional stitching, voiding, feathering and so on are all reserved for the cat itself.

A good photograph, as previously mentioned, is a fine starting point for an embroidery, but it should not be slavishly copied down to the last minutiae of detail. A photo can be useful in providing an accurate idea of proportions and markings, but for shading, shadowing and stitch direction it can be misleading. Good textbook illustrations (line drawings) are often a better guide. Trace and transfer your outline in the usual way, but rather than a smooth, inflexible line, try to create a softer, more fluid contour by suggesting a irregular line (see Fig 45). Include a rough idea of main markings, such as the spotted pattern of the back and rings on the tail, but do not try to include all the details of the face or other minor speckling. It is essential to have a variety of gauges of thread in the various colours needed, as certain very fine details, such as those on the nose and mouth, will need the finest of threads, while broad areas of fur can be worked in a fuller gauge.

Begin with the face. Work the pupils and then the irises of the eyes, surrounding them with slanting stitches in the direction of the fur. Take time to study the markings of your chosen subject closely. Look, too, at the way the fur behaves.

PLATE 57 (page 96 – 97)
The essential cat. It is said that the prophet Mohammed, called away to prayers on an occasion when his favourite cat was lying by his side, cut off the sleeve of his tunic rather than disturb the cat. Most cat owners will recognize this scenario! When relaxed, adult cats make superb models, apparently relishing the attention of pencil and pad. Whether working direct from your subject, or from a photograph, try to emphasize the multi-dimensional quality of the fur, which in places lies in opposing directions.

The stylized decorative motifs in this piece form a direct contrast to the realistic study of the cat. Eyes were symbols of fire and tokens of authority and the eye of Horus was a popular amulet. The anhk is the most famous of all Egyptian symbols — the hieroglyphic sign means 'life'. It has been suggested that the motif originated as a magic knot, signifying the 'thread of life' binding body and soul together; also known as the crux ansata, *it became a symbol of the Christian Coptic Church because of its cruciform shape. The scarab beetle* (Scarabaeus sacer) *was the image of self-creation as the Egyptians believed that it came into being of itself in a ball of dung.*

Most complex of the decorative motifs surrounding the cat is the winged disc. From the Fifth Dynasty of Egypt onwards a sun disc was placed between a pair of wings to create a solar symbol, also encompassing the concept of heaven.

The frieze along the top of the study, with its pendant beads, suggests a curtain framing the subject. The blue and yellow lotus flowers and buds were popular motifs on ceramics and wall paintings, and in paintings on wood. The lotus emerging from water was the symbol of the sun breaking through after the night. Various adaptations are shown in Fig 47
Embroidery shown life-size:
38 x 26cm (15 x 10¼in)

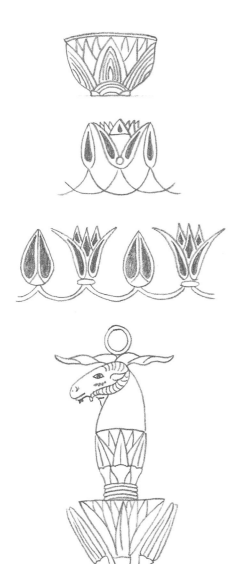

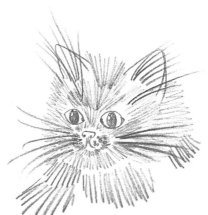

Fig 45 △

This long-haired kitten is all fur and little face!
To suggest the various layers of fur, try
working in two pencils, hard and soft. The soft,
lower image should be embroidered first and
the harder, superimposed lines of outer fur,
whiskers and so on stitched over the underlying
elements in a finer thread

Fig 46 △

When the direction of a cat's fur is analyzed
closely it becomes evident that the 'core' of the
study is not the nose itself, but rather the bridge
of the nose. Only a few lines of split stitch
run from the nose to the forehead, and the
stitches pirouette around them, from the bridge
to the cheek and eyes. Thereafter, the normal
flow of directional stitching gradually falls
back into place

Fig 47 △

The sacred lotus of the Nile was a
popular motif in ceramics, wall paintings and
so on. Its suitability as decoration for a bowl is
self-evident (top). Centre, the lotus and its buds
create a running frieze which has many uses,
whilst below it forms a column and plinth to
support a ram's head. The essentially two-
dimensional quality of much ancient Egyptian
art makes it easily adaptable as a design source
for embroidery

Cats are one of the rare subjects in embroidery which (in close up) do not adhere to the principle of every stitch falling away to the same 'core'. On the bridge of the nose the fur changes direction, down towards the nose, then upwards to the forehead, and pirouetting around itself to swing upwards and outwards to the inner corner of each eye. Using your finest thread work these features in split stitch and, having outlined the nose and mouth, continue split stitching in and around those features to create the nose, upper and lower cheeks, mouth and chin (Fig 46). When these very fine areas are complete, use radial *opus plumarium* in a broader gauge to continue working outwards to complete the head, reverting to a slightly elongated, fine split stitch for the ears.

Continue the directional stitching down into the body. Shadow line in broken straight stitches, imitating the 'sketched' effect of your outline. Work primary markings (if any) in dalmatian spots, adding those not transferred, and then build up the large fields of colour either singly, or in and around the spots. This is the point at which to use your own instinct with regard to shading; a photograph will often be too strongly lit to give the subtle effects which are required in embroidery. In Plate 57 a diffuse wash of grey mingles with the white beneath the chin and breastbone, rather than the hard shadow seen in a photo. When all the fields have been filled with the correct directional stitching, we can begin to 'soften' the portrait.

In a fine strand of each appropriate colour 'feather out' straight stitches across voids (for example between chin, neck and breast) and around the soft outlines of face, haunch and so on. Always work in the shade which represents the uppermost of any two fields, so that white, for instance, overlays grey where the leg lies across the main body. Finally, use similar, but longer, straight stitches to describe the long hairs in the ears, and finish off with whiskers and the all-important eye highlights.

This close attention to directional stitching (both radial and split) and softening of voids is essential to create a lifelike effect. Owls share some of the cat's characteristics in this connection (see Plate 60). Like cats, owls' large luminous eyes mean that it is difficult to establish a single 'core' for your stitching. In this case each eye is treated separately, a saucer-like dish of radial work in several strata built up around it which, abutting its neighbour, is softened by stitches first in one direction, then the other (see Fig 49). Again, like the cat, the soft quality of the owl's down is suggested by feathering out fine stitches along the breast and across the void between the face and throat, and careful attention must be paid to the directional work from neck to tail.

However accurate your directional work, it is possible to create entirely different effects depending upon how your finished embroidery is displayed. Plates 59.1 and 59.2 show the same detail of Plate 1, differently lit. A very black cat advancing towards the viewer in Plate 59.1 becomes a cat ethereally highlighted by moonlight in Plate 59.2. Even the whiskers, specially worked in black and grey to

Fig 48 △
With the imagined light source as shown, shadowing of 'furry' subjects can be effected by using straight stitches in the direction of the ultimate flow of the radial work. Here (bottom) the angled stitches suggest the shadow, while the hatched line simply outlines the rest of the motif

◁ *PLATE 59 (detail of Plate 1)*
With light shone horizontally across the figure of the stalking cat, the animal appears totally black (1), but when the light source is above the subject, individual stitches are highlighted (2), allowing them to stand out and so reveal tiny slivers of the background fabric – hey presto! – a black cat turns grey! Only through the magic of embroidery can such a transformation take place. Working in black on a pale background it would, of course, be useless to include a black shadow line. The separation of elements is therefore described (as it would be on a black background) by voiding. The expressive 'flip' of the cat's tail is particularly effective
Dimensions of cat:
3.5 x 9.5cm (1¼ x 3¾in)

PLATE 60 ▷

*The owl was the companion and symbol of the
Greek goddess Athene, famed for her wisdom
(and embroidery, see page 10), and giving rise
to the associated myth of the 'wise owl'. The
barn owl shown here* (Tyto alba) *has for
centuries been considered a bird of ill omen – its
prolonged eerie shriek can strike a chill into the
heart of the most hardened countryman.*

*In the fourteenth century Geoffrey Chaucer
called the bird a 'prophet of woe and mischance',
and yet it is so beautiful – and so beneficial to
farmers – that its serious decline in numbers
has been universally mourned. Fortunately
populations are now increasing once again,
due to careful husbandry of nesting sites and
food stocks.*

*The white and golden-buff plumage is
startlingly beautiful against a black background.
Careful voiding between each major feature –
facial disc, wing edge, legs and so on – is
continued to encompass the primary, secondary
and tertiary feathers, softened (as with the cat)
on the former, but left more distinct to
separate the feathers whose broad span allow
the bird an almost soundless flight.*

*The tree stump has been created using straight
stitched silk, overlaid with couched bouclé silk
and wool to form lichens and mosses*

11 x 15.5cm (4¼ x 6in)

◁ *Fig 49*

*Two 360-degree plates of feathers must be suggested
by complementary radial sweeps in directional*
opus plumarium *to create the inner face of the owl.
This makes the continuation of the radial
stitching difficult, as with the face of the cat, as the
angles of the stitches appear to be at odds.
Carefully working short strata, and softening these
with overlaid fine straight stitches, finally
achieves the desired effect*

catch the light, give a different effect under changed conditions (the technique for creating this silhouetted effect is discussed in Chapter Seven, page 113).

Cats have been popular motifs in many media for millennia. Egyptian wall paintings include those of tabby cats (also featured in bronze and stonework); the Romans favoured tabbies as subjects for mosaics; they have been sketched and painted endlessly – Leonardo da Vinci was fascinated by their grace and aggression; and (despite later association with witchcraft) they were found as symbols in the ancient Church. In the abbey on the island of Iona off the Scottish coast, founded by Saint Columba in 563, there is a stone-carved relief of a cat symbolizing contemplation (see Fig 50). It is remarkably similar to the interlaced cat motif in the Maaseik embroideries shown in Plate 61. Whatever the medium, the cat's sinuous, sensuous quality is never lost.

THE WILD HUNT

Above the cat in Plate 61, a handsome horse paws the ground impatiently, its body taut and ready for the gallop. The horse has played a part in mythology throughout history and its depiction in embroidery has been recorded since Classical times. In the *Iliad*, Homer describes Helen of Troy's skill as an embroideress and lists horses as among her many subjects (he also describes her silver work-basket on wheels). Viking tapestry and embroidery feature horses – including Odin's great eight-legged steed Sleipnir – and in the Bayeux Tapestry horses feature in both peace-time and warfare.

As a subject in the middle distance or in miniature, the horse can be approached with much the same elegance and simplicity of line as the unicorns in Plate 53 (page 90). However, as part of a large study, and where the horse features prominently in the foreground, it can be treated differently. Plate 62 shows a detail of Brithnoth's

◁ PLATE 61
Whilst fairly common in other media, cat studies are rare in English medieval embroidery. During the reconstruction of the Maaseik textiles (a project of some 300 hours duration) I came to feel that I knew the original artist almost personally. In my own studio, my cat is a constant companion – could it be that an Anglo-Saxon cat was the model for this sinuous interpretation? An eighth-century Celtic poet sums up the relationship perfectly:

I and Pangur Ban, my cat,
'Tis a like task we are at;
Hunting mice is his delight,
Hunting words I sit all night.

So in peace our tasks we ply,
Pangur Ban, my cat, and I;
In our arts we find our bliss,
I have mine and he has his

Dimensions of column:
3 x 4.5cm (1¼ x 1¾in)

Fig 50 △
Top: the outline of the stone cat from the monastic buildings at Iona bears a distinct likeness of form to the Maaseik textile cat motif (Plate 61). Both have been simplified here and background elements omitted

PLATE 62 (detail of Plate 50) ▷
To emphasize the antiquarian feel of this piece it has been worked on a broad evenweave linen, thicker than the lightweight evenweave cotton which is suitable for less substantial contemporary subjects. Working on fabrics with a lower 'count' means adapting the tension of your work, allowing the stitches to lie rather more loosely than usual. Pulling the stitches too taut distorts the weave. Also, stitches may have to lie slightly further apart (this is compensated for by the looser tension), in order that there are not too many stitches 'fighting' for a single intersection of warp and weft. Although all the techniques discussed are free (not counted) thread stitches it is still important to be aware of the weave qualities of your background fabric
Dimensions of detail shown:
8.25 x 9.5cm (3¼ x 3¾in)

horse (from Plate 50, page 85). Unlike a cat, whose soft, multi-directional fur hides the real contours of its head, the bone structure of the horse, together with other very short-haired animals, is at the heart of a successful study. A strong outline, together with an indication of the contours of the eye socket, cheek-bones and nostril, is an essential framework within which to build the face. Once this has been completed, use several shades of the same basic colour – in this case golden brown, from dark to light – to follow the contours in directional stitching, dark first, then broadening into the larger fields of paler brown. Both the eye and nostril should be highlighted, the latter to suggest depth and moistness.

The contours of the red deer stag's head (*Cervus elaphus*) in Plate 63 have been built up using the same principles, although the main infill technique is split stitching. The 'core' of the work is the soft, moist muzzle of the animal, the stitches ultimately falling back towards it. The glory of this study, of course, is the deer's magnificent antlers. Sporting ten fine tines, the young stag is at its prime, about five years old; antlers are shed annually and regrow for the new season's rut, each year becoming larger and more complex. Using carefully contoured split stitching, light above and darker below, with a shadow line, the antlers are built up tine by tine, blending smoothly together at intersections. The pedicles (platforms from which the antlers emerge) are worked in detail, as they are an important aspect of the deer's unique physiognomy, and the large, expressive eyes given extra prominence by a larger than usual highlight.

In Celtic mythology the chariot of the goddess Flidass is drawn by a deer, and stags were thought to be able to pass from this to the otherworld, and to escort souls safely on their journeys. Herne the Hunter, an elusive figure in mythology – sometimes the leader of the Wild Hunt, a ghostly pack of horsemen and their hounds; sometimes a benign woodland character – wears antlers, identifying himself with the nobility and strength of the stag. Symbolically, the deer appears always to be benevolent and a study such as Plate 63 could be miniaturized still further to create a delightful good-luck pendant.

In the cold light of reality, nature's most beautiful creatures often seem to be the victim of the huntsman. Like the stag, the hare must be fleet of foot if she is to escape her pursuers, and Plate 64 shows the agility of the 'mad March hare' as she scampers across the wide East Anglian landscape. According to

Fig 51 ▽
Versatile split stitch:
1 Linear split stitch used to create the strong contours of the stag's antlers
2 Radial split stitch defines and describes the contours of the head
3 A combination of both suggests both the erect, rigid quality of the ear, whilst also giving the effect of its soft, downy texture

◁ PLATE 63
As in larger studies, it is important to establish the light source within your microcosm of design, and shadow line accordingly; in this case, as with other animal portraits, allowing the shadow to take the form of a broken line, radiating in the direction of the animal's coat where stitch forms terminate in a open, rather than linear, strata (see Fig 51).
Deep shadows in black suggest the funnel-shaped inner ears, while the grey collar around the stag's neck is partly shadow, partly integral markings, as are the two distinctive light spots under the animal's chin
10cm (4in) round, including frame

Fig 52 ▷

The angled birds in flight (top) are worked
very simply. Work a rather splayed-out capital
'M'. Create a wedge shape by adding a stitch
as shown to the left-hand members, followed by
a second to the right. A couple of straight
stitches at the centre of the 'M' suggest the
bird's body. The process can be reversed to give
a bird flying in the opposite direction

PLATE 64 ▷

The 'hare-in-the-moon' is an almost universal
myth, occurring in Mexico, South Africa, the
Far East, India and other places, and it is easy
to see the contour of a hare in the moon's
features. Certain of the native American
peoples believed that the Great Hare
Manabazho lived in the moon with the Great
Spirit Manitou. A widespread belief was that
after the flood only one pair of humans
survived on the earth, and all fire was
extinguished. Many animals tried to reach the
moon, where these guardians kept fires
burning. Eventually the water spider spun a
magic thread which she wove into a bowl, and
so carried an ember back to the earth. The
spider and her magic thread will be discussed
further in Chapter Seven. In China, figures
and embroideries of hares were worked
particularly during the Moon Festival
Embroidery shown life-size:
23.5 x 24cm (9¼ x 9½in)

Julius Caesar, the hare was an important animal to the ancient Britons, and Boudicca released a hare at the start of each campaign. The Teutonic goddess Eostre (from whom we derive the name of Easter) was sometimes depicted as hare-headed, and her attendant hare gave birth to an egg every spring representing new life. From these legends our own Easter eggs and the Easter bunny were born. Like the horse and the stag, the hare also appears on the Bayeux Tapestry.

Many of the same techniques which were employed in working the cat (Plate 57) are used again here (Plate 64). Seen in profile, it is easier to establish the directional flow of stitches on the hare, but very careful attention should be paid to contouring them on the front and hindlegs and haunches – the animal is in action and the flexing of the appropriate muscles is all-important to capture the reality of that movement. The legs furthest from the viewer should be worked in a distinctly darker shade and voids feathered over to suggest perspective successfully.

The overall perspective of the study places the hare in close up, whilst allowing the landscape to recede into the extreme distance. Whilst the speed of the animal is suggested by the low-growing grasses curving towards the running hare – caught in the slipstream of her flight – the stillness of the early spring morning is emphasized by the upright stitches of the distant stand of trees and broad horizontal blue-and-white swathes of sky and cloud. Apart from the hare, the only movement is the lazy flapping of the seagulls overhead, and it is possible to suggest these birds in some detail with just a few stitches. By working a three-dimensional 'M' shape in black silk, bisected with a straight stitch for the body, and white and black banding on the wings, the distinctive high-flying silhouette of inland seagulls seeking an easy meal can be successfully captured. This process is set out in detail in Fig 52.

HELEN
STEVENS

PLATE 65 ▷

Living close to nature, the ancients believed in all things being connected by an intricate web, and the smallest of creatures were able to vibrate that web and so play an integral part in the magical world which our ancestors felt all around them. The beetle's ability both to run swiftly and to fly put it in an almost unique category. One tenth-century Anglo-Saxon riddle certainly seems to describe just such a creature: 'I saw fleet-foot flit the trail'. The green tiger beetle is an insect mainly of heathland where it is a ferocious predator of smaller bugs. Using silk recreates the iridescent shimmer of the wing cases perfectly; or cotton could be twisted with a blending filament to give a similar effect. Attractive insects make delightful subjects for brooches or other jewellery items
Insect approximately:
3.75 x 2cm (1½ x ¾in)

PLATE 66 ▷

Harvest mice (Micromys minutus) are the weavers and embroiderers of the rodent world. Late in the spring, the female builds her nest, weaving grasses and leaves (still attached to their mother plant) into a living hammock. This she fills with dried, shredded leaves, finally camouflaging the whole nest with an intricate interweaving of more living grasses to create a hidden nursery for her young. The summer is spent high in the swaying grasses. During the autumn harvest, mice retreat to hedgerows and shrubland where they become ground-dwelling, depending on berries, seeds and insects for their sustenance. Unlike the field mouse in Plate 58, the harvest mouse has a truly prehensile tail and so its coiled interlace with the parsley stem is entirely naturalistic! As the mouse climbs the stems its slight weight curves them to once side – remember to exploit the trick of using such realism when designing your work
13 x 18cm (5 x 7in)

Embroidery really is an amazing medium. From a scene capturing several square miles of landscape we can move effortlessly to a study whose subject is just 2cm (¾in) in length! Whilst the ancient Egyptians venerated the scarab – a type of dung beetle – for its mystic attributes (Plate 57), it can hardly be said to be an attractive creature in its own right. There are, however, many beetles which are truly beautiful and which translate well into detailed embroideries, to be used either as adjuncts to a larger work, or featured individually as decorative motifs, or even incorporated into jewellery.

The green tiger beetle (*Cicindela campestris*), shown in Plate 65, is a magically iridescent little creature, no doubt just the kind thought to be the coach-horse of Queen Mab of the fairies. The fairy coach 'drawn with a team of little atomies … the cover, of the wings of grasshoppers; the traces, of the smallest spider's web' (Shakespeare) was said to be drawn across men's noses as they lay asleep! The head, thorax and wing cases are worked first in satin stitch, incorporating two dalmatian dog spots into each wing case. Chevron stitch in black is worked for the upper segments of each leg, and infilled with fine gold thread, and slightly thicker gold thread is then couched around the body and the spots. Straight stitches complete the legs and feet, with black antennae, couched in gold to add a final spectacular dazzle. Tiny seed stitches in yellow and white complete the design.

The addition of 'special effects' to give added enchantment to embroidery has always been a feature of the art. Pearls on the arcaded architecture of the Maaseik textiles (Plates 27, 61 and 70) focus the eye upon the activity within each arch, the magic of 'or nue' and other goldwork techniques in medieval embroidery, and shisha mirror sequins in Jacobean work, all of which bear witness to the joys of artistic licence. In Plate 66 ice-blue sequins and tiny glass seed beads create stylized snowflakes adding a sense of the esoteric to an otherwise entirely naturalistic study. Leaves, berries and the spiky dead-heads of the cow parsley are all dusted with a light covering of snow in the shape of tiny speckling and seed stitches (see Plate 33, page 57) and the mouse worked similarly to Plate 58. The fantastic quality added to the picture by the falling snowflakes is achieved by working them at random – overlaying other features in places – and making them an integral part of the whole by drawing the mouse's beady eye directly towards the nearest flake (see the discussion of this technique on page 52).

CHAPTER SEVEN

SACRED PLACES

A church and a chapitile wonderly wel y-bild,
With niches on everiche half and bellyche y-corven;
With crotchetes on corners, with knottes of gold,
With gay glitering glas glowyng as the sunne …

The Crede of Piers Plowman
Fourteenth Century

HELEN
STEVENS

 NRICHED with gold, silver and silk, my Lady's embroidery was almost complete. She blew out her candle. The Story-teller whispered low:

'One more tale to tell of a heart bound by the threads of true love. On the faraway island of Crete, where the sun burns brightly, there was a dark, dank labyrinth. Fair Ariadne's lover, brave Theseus, had vowed to kill the beast which dwelt in the maze, but no man had entered the labyrinth and survived – for no man could find his way out. The goddess of love, Aphrodite, whispered to Ariadne in a dream to give Theseus a skein of her finest, brightest silk, that he might let it out behind him as he entered the maze – and so find his way back to his true love. Ariadne did as she was bid, and Theseus strode into the meandering passages, paying out his precious lifeline. Of the sights he saw there he never spoke, but the beast was killed, Theseus returned and the lovers sailed away…'

PLATE 68 △

'E' Here the concept of the 'tree of life' has been combined with the idea of a maze, with the 'web of life' at its core, the motifs designed to echo the art nouveau movement. Stem stitch in brown outlines the labyrinthine trunks and branches of the tree, each line whipped with a fine gold thread to create the effect of a narrow, twisted cord. Stylized leaves are worked in two shades of silk, and blossom suggested by small faux pearls and seed beads in pink and ivory. At the base of the work are roughly cut citrines. The shadows cast by the beads create a pleasing depth to the piece, which is worked on a background fabric painted with dilute fabric dye to give a variation of shades, pale blue at the base of the piece, deepening towards the top, like a summer sky

10 x 13.5cm (4 x 5¼in)

ALL ROADS LEAD TO…

The labyrinth or maze exerts an almost universal fascination. It appears in the most ancient civilizations, from the Egyptians and all the early Mediterranean cultures to Oriental, Indian and Tibetan creeds. In Britain it was used by the pagans before appearing as a symbol in medieval Christianity. At the heart of the maze lies the heart's desire, the spiritual home, which can only be reached by overcoming the complexities and hardships of life – the monsters of the subconscious. The only safe way to enter and subsequently escape from eternity in the labyrinth is to use the 'golden thread' which connects body to soul. Retrace the thread to the entrance and you are back in the mortal realm; lose it, cut it, or deliberately abandon it and there is no way out, for the heart of the maze is in the otherworld.

The origins of Glastonbury Tor are uncertain. It has been a sacred place since prehistoric times, and at some time a maze of walkways was cut around the sides of the great hill, requiring the faithful to take a meandering path up its steep inclines to the top. The magic of the tor and the ruins of Glastonbury Abbey below inspired the landscape in Plate 67. During daylight, the views both of the tor and from its summit are spectacular, but at night the mystical beauty of the place is eerie and spellbinding. During the crisp, moonlit nights of winter the silhouettes of frost-bound trees sparkle, moonlight throws stark shadows across the ancient masonry and the tor rises mysterious and beckoning against the starry sky.

The contours of the tor, undulating with the ancient maze route, are worked simply by adapting the straight horizontal techniques for landscape work (discussed in Chapter Three, Plate 31 and Fig 22). Successive rounded plateaux, each rising above the next, have been worked in differing shades of dull green, no two similar shades abutting, with careful voiding between each section. Both the tower of St Michael's church (on the summit of the tor) and the ruins of the abbey below are worked in bold etching, dotting and dashing (see Appendix A, page 129). The trees are worked in converging straight stitches, threads becoming finer towards the extremities of the branches and twigs as their tracery becomes more delicate.

Legend holds that Joseph of Arimathea (who brought the Holy Grail to Glastonbury) arrived in the valley below the tor, footsore and weary. Believing that he had reached the end of his journey, he struck his staff into the ground, where it took root and grew into a fine hawthorn bush which, despite the fact that it was winter, burst into flower. The ancient tree, or its direct descendant, still stands – and still blooms every Christmas – hence the spring-like buds and blossoms surrounding the wintry landscape. The hawthorn branch frames the picture, without being part of the scene, and so it was important that the moonbeams shining through the arches of the ruined abbey appeared to be *behind* this framework, whilst in front of the other elements of the picture.

These long beams of moonlight were a challenge. In my original sketch it was simple enough to suggest moonlight, but translating this into embroidery required careful preparation. When transferring the design onto fabric the ultimate position of the moonbeams must be indicated; this cannot be shown on the fabric itself, as it

◁ *PLATE 67 (page 110 – 111)*
A Glastonbury romance. The strange, unearthly effect of moonlight can be effectively captured in embroidery, especially on a black background, which lends itself perfectly to the deep brooding qualities of the shadows and the sparkling highlights of the stars. Above the tor the night sky is suggested by a sinuous ribbon of moonlit cloud, worked in horizontal stitches of dove grey, and a small scattering of stars, forming the constellation of the 'Lady's Wain' (see the goddess Frigg page 66), today more commonly called Ursa Minor, the Little Bear. A pathway from the foot of the tor, worked in green cotton, meanders toward the abbey ruins, leaving broad swathes of black on either side of it, suggesting the unknown, unseen otherworld.

Echoing the fantasy of the design by surrounding the work with a misty grey or blue window mount would be an effective way of disguising the outer edges of the moonbeams. Be careful when framing a piece like this not to overwhelm the design with too heavy a frame, and be scrupulous in your checking to see that no specks of dust, lint or stray strands of silk are left on the black background. A useful way of picking up these irritating bits and pieces is to wind a small amount of sticky tape, adhesive side outwards, around your finger, and dab the surface of the fabric. Do not touch the embroidery itself as delicate stitching may lift and fragment
Embroidery shown life-size:
43 x 29cm (17 x 11½in)

. . . .

Fig 53 ▷

*My original sketch for Plate 67 (minus trees
and other elements) showed the angles
of the moonlight flooding through the arches
of the abbey ruins*

Fig 54 ▽

*By working out the ultimate position of the
window mount (1), I was able to judge where
to terminate the moonbeams in such a way that
the end of each long stitch would be hidden.
The field of the moonlight was outlined (2)
and dots marked around the outside of
the mount line (3). As long as the stitches
terminated at the point of the dots, the
moonlight would appear to extend beyond
the parameters of the landscape*

would be impossible to disguise later. The extremities of the study's dimensions (where the window mount will be positioned) must be determined and a line drawn about 1.25cm (¹/₂in) outside this dimension. This can be transferred onto the fabric, after the main design, using a white tailor's pencil. Calculating the angle of the beams from the original sketch, pencil in dots to show the ultimate destination of each long stitch. By taking the stitches to this outer dimension, it is certain that their 'ends' will be covered by the window mount (Figs 53 and 54).

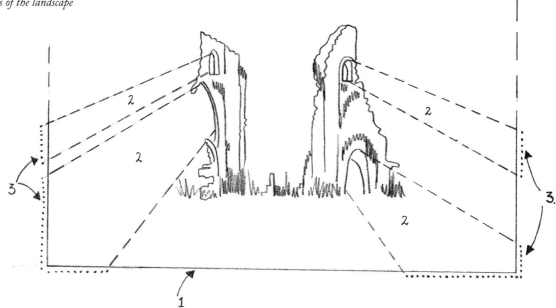

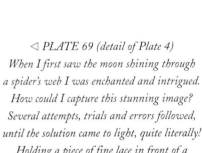

◁ *PLATE 69 (detail of Plate 4)*
When I first saw the moon shining through
a spider's web I was enchanted and intrigued.
How could I capture this stunning image?
Several attempts, trials and errors followed,
until the solution came to light, quite literally!
Holding a piece of fine lace in front of a
spotlight I analyzed the way in which the
light fell through the fine tracery, refined the
design still further, and the puzzle of the
cobweb was solved.
When you spot a new and exciting idea, make
a note of it right away, and a rough sketch too,
if possible. If you are not sure how to translate
the image, begin with something simpler and
work your way towards your goal in easy
stages. Several of my own techniques have come
about in this way, such as the honeycomb
technique for dragonfly wings, bumble bees in
flight, fish scales and, of course, spider's webs!
Dimensions of detail shown:
10.25 x 13cm (4 x 5in)

The moonbeams are created by strands of cellophane, separated from a colourless blending filament. The landscape elements of the picture were worked first. Using a very fine needle, take long stitches from the ruined archways to the dots outside the main framework. The hawthorn is then worked *over* the moonbeams, taking care not to stitch through any cellophane strands, which would, of course, fracture and break loose.

Special effects suggested by moonlight can be spectacular. In Plate 4 (pages 8–9), a spider's web is silhouetted across the moon, and the cat's whiskers in Plate 59 (1 and 2) are similarly emphasized and thrown into relief. Plate 69 shows this process in detail. The moon, worked in pink-silver horizontal stitching and outlined in silver metallic thread, is embroidered first. Then the spider's web is worked across it in the usual way (see Appendix A, page 127), taking care that stitches taken through the moon are not drawn too tightly, and do not distort the underlying work. Each area

PLATE 70 ▷
*The idea of the puzzle maze was enjoyed by the
Anglo-Saxons, in miniature form. The two
interlaced zoomorphic beasts at the centre of
this piece are both a puzzle and a joke: a visual
riddle. At first glance the maze-like form of the
goldwork suggests two perfectly symmetrical
designs, interlaced and aligned along a central
mirror. The tongue of the beast facing to the
right emerges from the mouth, interlaces with
the animal's own neck and the body of its
companion, before neatly turning into its own
tail! One would expect the tongue of the other
beast to behave likewise – but not so!
It emerges, interlaces and entwines and finally
finishes up somewhere else completely.
(This can be seen more easily in Plate 18,
Chapter One, page 33, where the motif is
shown during working.) This was clearly not a
simple mistake of design – the other 100 yards
or so of pure gold interlace on the Maaseik
textile is impeccable – but to the Anglo-Saxon
mind would be seen as making a joke at the
expense of the art 'establishment', whose
interlace was almost invariably immaculate*
Dimensions of arcade:
7.5 x 6.5cm (3 x 2½in)

of the web which crosses the disc is then lowlighted in a fine black thread by working an exact replica of each stitch immediately *below* it, effectively creating a 'negative' image. Working black whiskers on a black cat, the technique is reversed – a fine white or grey highlight line is stitched immediately *above* each whisker.

The spider and her web are sacred to many cultures. Several African tribes share the belief of the native Americans that fire was brought to earth by means of a spider's thread (see Chapter Six, page 106). The Loango people take the tale a step further: the silken thread is tossed into the sky by the wind, and the woodpecker climbs up and pecks holes in the sky – the stars. Then man climbs up and fetches fire. The medicine men of aboriginal Australia trace very similar stories back to the 'dream time'. The Classical figure of Penelope, wife of Odysseus, is sometimes represented as a spider; each day she wove her tapestry (web), but refused to cut the silk as it represented the thread of her missing husband's life. For twenty years she stitched on, until Odysseus returned home safely.

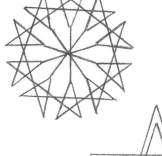

◁ *Fig 55*
*Penelope's Web (left) is an ancient symbol for
the web of life and a sign of protection, being
formed by ten mystic pentacles. The unbroken
life force, represented by the single uncut thread
forming the lone pentacle, is magnified
ten times, and extra protection afforded by the
twenty outward spokes of the web*

… HOME

However magical the journey, however wondrous the places and people visited, coming home has a unique enchantment. As needlework from the Jacobean period onwards testifies, working an embroidery of your own home is a rewarding project, and the finished piece is likely to be treasured for generations. For this purpose a good photograph is essential – it allows you to be confident of perspective and proportion – but it need not preclude artistic licence. If there are aspects of your garden at the back which cannot be seen from the best angle for the house, move them to the front! (see *The Timeless Art of Embroidery*).

Your home's surroundings may be more magical than you thought. Many old houses were built beside copses, rivers and ponds, not just because of the practical advantages, but also to benefit from the protection of the spirits of those places. Certain trees were planted to bring good luck and prosperity to the home, whilst others reflected the occupations of those within. The spindle tree (*Euonymus europaeus*)

Fig 56 ▽

The spindle tree has a distinctive, twiggy outline in winter, and a fragile tracery of blossom and foliage in spring and summer. Its very hard wood was once whittled and turned to form the spindles of the 'wise women', a tradition remembered in the tale of the Sleeping Beauty. The Wicked Fairy decrees that the Princess' life would be forfeit if she was pricked with a spindle – as we know, the curse was thwarted!

◁ *PLATE 71*

This little study, inspired by my own house, captures the essence of 'Home, Sweet, Home', the type of image so beloved of the Victorian sampler. The roof has been worked in a broad laddering stitch, the wistaria clambering over and along it, overhanging windows and clambering up to the chimney. Tall spikes of delphiniums and foxgloves cluster at the sides of the house, while the black and sky-blue windows suggest the reflective qualities of glass, and the idea that there is something inside the façade. The shades of the sky are also reflected in the water of the pond, though rather than worked in fine sleave silk it has been stitched using a fine 2/1T silk thread in similar shades
14.75 x 13.5cm (5³⁄₄ x 5¹⁄₄in)

PLATE 72 (detail of Plate 47) ▷
Home for the wild boar family is shown here, snug against the haystacks. The smooth-leaved elm (Ulmus carpinifolia) *is a narrow, towering tree often planted specifically on farmland in earlier centuries. In East Anglia it was often pollarded (cut off at about head height) to produce a crop of strong, straight sticks, traditionally used as pea and bean poles. This elm has a distinctive outline, which sets it apart from the English or wych elm; strong, thick boughs emerge almost vertically from the central trunk, separating out into smaller branches which turn down at the end. Work the seed stitched leaves on the upper surface of each twig first, followed by the lower, to achieve this terminal shape accurately*
Dimensions of detail shown:
13 x 16.5cm (5 x 6½in)

PLATE 73 ▷
Over the centuries ancient flintwork requires patching and mending, and all manner of stones are added by hands less skilled than the original craftsman. Bits of stone and masonry, house bricks and mortar all jumble together to create a marvellous texture and blend of colours. Work your dotting stitches randomly to achieve this effect, allowing grey, flinty colours to predominate, which will throw the occasional terracotta stitch into relief. The meandering brown path leading to the porch doorway draws the eye into the picture and is echoed by the lower region of the sky, suggesting a pathway into infinity
13.5 x 11cm (5¼ x 4¼in)

can be found beside homes which once housed 'spinsters', usually unmarried girls who made their living spinning yarn (and the occasional spell), using spindles made from the tree's dense, hard wood; and the low-growing wych hazel (*Hamamelis mollis*) (Plate 71) was the favourite tree of water diviners, or 'dowsers' – the word 'wych' is Old English for pliant, a prerequisite for the dowsing rods.

Plate 71 shows shrubs growing beyond, next to and scrambling over the cottage. The hazel bushes are at the rear of the composition, and worked first (frameworks of branches, 'clothed' with seed stitched leaves). They are followed in order of working by the more colourful shrubs and flowers to their front, and only after the house itself has been fully completed is the wistaria embroidered over the underlying features; no background fabric shows through the work, and the close

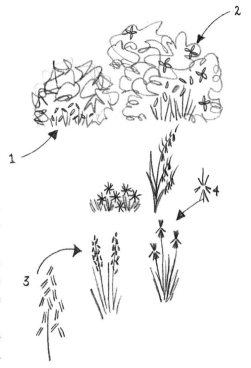

Fig 57 ▷
*Distant, impressionistic flowers are a useful
addition to any landscape, quickly worked and
yet very effective.
In the far distance, single seed stitches (1) or
groups of a few together (2) suggest any
number of flowers or blossoms, according to
their chosen colour. Foxgloves or other tall,
spiked plants are suggested by straight
stitches surmounted by groups of twin seed
stitches (3) whilst irises are created by an
elongated rosette of seed stitches, thinning at
each side to create the appropriate
distinctive outline (4)*

proximity of shrub and brickwork is successfully suggested. The pond, too, requires to be worked in a particular order. First the plants growing in the water are completed, then the various shades of blue worked around them, suggesting the open and shadowed waters. The upright grasses fringing the pool are then worked over the water in the foreground, and over the horizontally stitched lawn to the rear. Similarly in Plate 72 (a detail of Plate 47) the wildflowers around the haystacks are superimposed when the larger features are complete. In both cases the flowers are treated impressionistically – dashes and dots of vibrant colour are all that the eye recognizes in the far distance (see Fig 57).

A spiritual home – such as a local parish church – is also a lovely subject. Plate 73 shows the tiny Anglo-Saxon church of St Mary the Virgin at Cranwich in Norfolk. Thatched, and with the distinctive round tower of pre-conquest England, it nestles

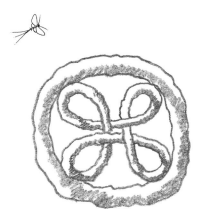

Fig 58 △
The stone knot high in the walls of Cranwich
church tower

amid trees and grasses, seemingly a million miles from the busy road which runs nearby. Below the arched window at the top of the tower is another, smaller, window with a fascinating design. Carved in stone is an endless 'knot' (sketched in Fig 58), the ancient symbol of continuity, eternity, longevity – the thread of life, with no beginning and no end. A pagan concept embraced, adapted and incorporated into the Christian Church, the silken strand which, like the labyrinth, stands for the tortuous path that leads to enlightenment.

SANCTUARY

Nature's view of the spider's web is more down to earth. 'Is it dangerous, or is it edible?' is the only question in the hedgehog's mind (Plate 74). With few natural predators, the hedgehog (*Erinaceus europaeus*) seems to possess a high level of confidence, and is a noisy animal for its size, both during feeding and courting. Its sharp spines are an effective deterrent to hunters, and it is a proficient swimmer and climber, and a fast runner.

This small study typifies many of the practical aspects of embroidery which we have discussed. It could be designed from either a photo or sketched from life; hedgehogs are frequent garden visitors and not shy of modelling, especially if

provided with a dish of cat food! The design tells a simple story, the picture is framed by its component parts (almost stylized on its black background), and the main subject treated realistically, fur softened and feathered, eye focused. The animal is at home in its environment – the picture 'works'.

In landscape work we have also discussed what makes a successful picture – composition, depth, perspective – and in Plate 75 there is an element of mystery as a dew-drenched mist rises from the water meadows surrounding Ely Cathedral in Cambridgeshire. Called the 'ship of the Fens', the great building towers majestically over the flat countryside, emerging from the surrounding trees like a forecastle amid billowing waves. The eye is focused on the building, and yet invited to explore the rest of the landscape – the sky at dawn, peachy apricot at lower levels, softening to a mere trace of blue above, with a suggestion of wheeling birds to add movement.

The Fens of Cambridgeshire are a cradle of early English embroidery. The *Liber Eliensis*, a medieval chronicle and inventory of the cathedral's treasures, numbers many fine embroideries among its collection, made locally and bequeathed, bought or simply given to the establishment. The names of surrounding villages such as Coveney, Witcham and Witchford bear witness to their inhabitants' knowledge of 'cunning ways', and it is documented that a certain Aelswith, granddaughter of Brithnoth of Essex (see Chapter Five), maintained a school of embroidery in Coveney, much of whose output found its way to the abbey. Life was hard in the unforgiving Fens, but Anglo-Saxon women were not daunted by hardship. The literature of the time describes them as either 'shield maidens', sharing and bearing the responsibilities of their menfolk (or taking such burdens upon their own 'spinster' shoulders) or 'peace weavers', using their feminine qualities of perception, tolerance and conciliation to smooth over and knit together rifts in the social fabric of their society.

Everyone needs a home, a haven where we can feel safe and secure. Embroidery, certainly amateur embroidery, taken in its literal meaning – work undertaken 'for the love' of the art – is a medium most frequently enjoyed in the peace and tranquillity of the home. Those of us who, indeed, love the art are maintaining traditions which pre-date recorded history, echo myths of the Creation and hide secrets into which, for millennia, only the initiated were allowed. There are lessons bound up in the magic of thread which are vital in

Fig 59 ▷
*The study of Ely Cathedral is built up
sequentially, layer upon layer:
1 The cathedral building
2 The trees are worked first in tracery and then
clothed with foliage
3 Ranks of grasses and flowers sweep towards
the viewer
4 The rising mist is overlaid in very fine
horizontal stitching*

◁ *PLATE 74*
*Detailed chevron stitch worked in three colours
– dark grey below, lighter above, each stitch
run through with a white, protruding core –
gives the hedgehog its quality of solidity. The
rolling, ground-hugging gait of this delightful
creature places it firmly on the floor of its
woodland, hedgerow or garden home, where
leaf mould, moss and debris hide a variety of
foods – slugs, beetles, snails. A dish of cat food
is an acceptable contribution from a grateful
gardener – avoid the traditional bread and
milk as it results in severe indigestion. If you
are fortunate enough to be able to observe a
hedgehog closely, or even stroke it (beware
of fleas!), note the change in texture between
the strong, spiky spines and the soft fur
of the face and underbelly. Emphasize this in
your embroidery by feathering the fur over
the spines where appropriate. The placing of
the highlight in the eye is strategic – make
sure that contact is realized between the main
and bit players of this scene! (see Fig 21,
Chapter Three)
14 x 9.5cm (5½ x 3¾in)*

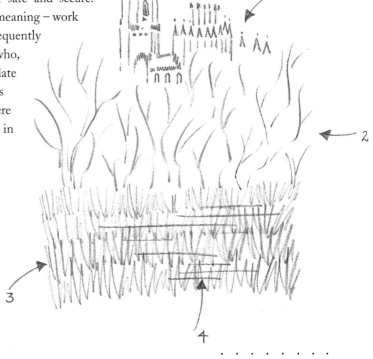

HELEN
STEVENS

◁ *Fig 60*
The Cornucopia, or Horn of Plenty, is another
embodiment of the yin-yang concept.
Male and female, hollow and yet full, it is
the source of life. Like the Grail, it is the
Cauldron of the Wise, and at its core begins
the Thread of Life

◁ *PLATE 75*
Ely Cathedral. During the Middle Ages,
and until a century or so ago, the Isle of Ely
was truly an island in the Fens. On a wet
spring morning, as the mist rises, it retains
much of its mystery.
In this study the foreground sweeps towards the
viewer, rank upon rank of features
superimposed upon each other. The cathedral is
embroidered first, followed by the framework of
the trees. These are the only two elements
transferred onto the background fabric – the
leafing of the trees, the advancing swathes of
grass (dotted with white and yellow
wildflowers) and suggestion of water is all
applied freehand. Let the spirit of the art have
sway without preconceived notions of how the
piece will ultimately appear
Embroidery shown life-size:
19 x 24cm (7½ x 9½in)

today's materialistic and violent world; and we must, like Anglo-Saxon women, decide if we are to be shield maidens or peace weavers – or a little of both. For the peace weaver must wield something of the strength of the shield maiden, if she is to be heard above the din of the twenty-first century.

Homes are not only essential to humans; nature walks a tightrope between survival and destruction as habitats dwindle, rainforests disappear, the seas are polluted and even the sky no longer protects us from the sun. The time has surely come for us to use the new 'web' to bring the world together in the search for solutions. Our generation must not be the one that breaks the thread of life on earth.

What can we do? Continue to spread the word of the interlaced, interwoven strands that bind the universe together – but above all use and enjoy the magical art of embroidery to portray our still beautiful, spellbinding world. And remember, it's the thread that binds the spell.

AR across the snow-swept Fens the great abbey bells began to ring for primes. My Lady clipped her shears and needles onto her chatelaine, put her embroidery into its basket and walked softly towards her chamber. The Story-teller threw another log onto the fire, wrapped himself in his cloak and lay down on the bench. He twisted a few inches of discarded silk into a bow, and slipped it inside his tunic.

APPENDIX A
BASIC TECHNIQUES

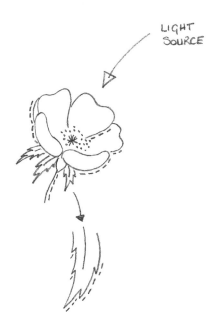

LIGHT SOURCE

Fig A1 △
The imagined light source within the picture is coming from the top right-hand corner. All elements opposite to the light source should be shadow lined, as indicated by the hatched line

PLATE 76 ▷
These techniques, including the use of simple radial stitching, opus plumarium and dalmatian dog, are all fully explored in The Embroiderer's Countryside *Embroidery shown life-size:*
20.5 x 28cm (8 x 11in)

Techniques explored here are fully explained in *The Embroiderer's Countryside* and *The Embroiderer's Country Album* (see Select Bibliography, page 142 for details). Conventional stitches, such as satin stitch, and the like, have not been included as these may be found in any good embroidery textbook.

Plates 76 and 77 are composite designs in the form of samplers which illustrate many of the techniques mentioned below. Where appropriate, the individual motifs are reproduced as line drawings to simplify the directions.

OUTLINING AND VOIDING
These two techniques define and differentiate between planes of stitching.

Outlining – Also referred to as shadow lining. Only used in work on a pale background. Imagine where the light is coming from *inside* your picture and work a fine line of stitching, in black, along the opposite edge of each motif (see Fig A1).

Voiding – Used in work on a pale or dark background. Where one element of a design overlaps another, leave a narrow line void of stitching. The line should be approximately the width of the gauge of thread used.

RADIAL STITCHING
Close ranks of stitching apparently emanating from a single core and describing a wedge, arc or full circle. Stitches are taken from the outside edge of the motif inwards, where necessary disappearing behind their neighbours. Two or more strata of radial stitching are necessary to build up a broad motif (see Fig A2).

OPPOSITE ANGLE EMBROIDERY
Used where a motif reflexes, eg, on a leaf or petal. The reverse of the subject should be worked at the same, but opposite, angle to the existing radial stitching (see Fig A3).

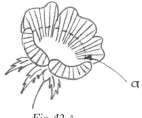

Fig A2 △
Radial lines shown suggest only about one in four of the stitches needed to work the motif. Hatched line 'a' shows the approximate point at which the second stratum of stitching should begin

Fig A3 △
Opposite angle embroidery is used where a leaf or other motif reflexes. Note the angle of stitches on one surface of the motif and exactly reverse it for the other side

HELEN
STEVENS

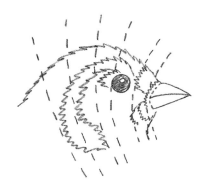

Fig A4 △
Opus plumarium *is so called because it imitates the way in which a bird's feathers lie on its body. Here, radial strata roughly equate to the markings on the bird's head – the eye should always be worked at an opposite angle to the main field of the embroidery*

Fig A5 ▽
The darker hatching (1) indicates the inner core of the work. The surrounding wedges of radial work (2) are worked smoothly into the core. Open arrows indicate the direction in which individual stitches should be taken. The hatched arrow is a reminder that the whole motif should sweep outwards from the body of the animal

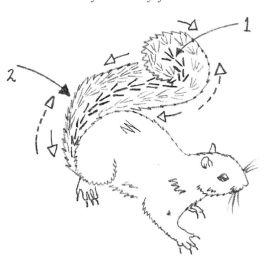

OPUS PLUMARIUM

Literally 'feather work'. Following the principal of radial stitching, as many strata as necessary blend together to fill large areas (see Fig A4).

DALMATIAN DOG TECHNIQUE

The method of incorporating features within *opus plumarium* to form a single smooth plane: ie, work black spots and then embroider a white dog around them. Ensure that the elements to be included are worked at the same angle of stitching as the embroidery which is to surround them. Blend together smoothly without outline or voiding (see butterfly in Plate 75).

RIVER STITCH

Method of working *opus plumarium* when the field to be covered sweeps from one direction to another, such as on a squirrel's tail. Work a core of embroidery as a narrow band of *opus plumarium* and on either side work fan shaped wedges of radial stitching, increasing and decreasing the angle of the wedge as necessary to describe the curve (see Fig A5).

SNAKE STITCH

Used to fill a field too narrow for *opus plumarium* and too wide for stem stitch. Beginning at the centre of a motif, work satin stitch first towards one extremity and then the other (see Fig A6).

TICKING

Short stitches overlaying *opus plumarium* worked at exactly the same angle as the underlying work, but taken in the opposite direction. Often used to describe the fine markings on the heads and underparts of birds.

STUDDING

Short stitches overlaying *opus plumarium* worked at the opposite angle to the underlying stitches. Often used when scale does not permit the use of dalmatian dog technique (see miniature woodpecker in medallion in Plate 75).

SHOOTING STITCH

A long straight stitch taken in the opposite direction to underlying radial work. Used to create subtle streaks on petals, etc.

LADDERING

A basic technique to illustrate chequerboard markings. Fill the field to be worked with satin or, if necessary, radial work. Using a contrasting shade, weave backwards and forwards through the existing stitches (without going through the background fabric), leaving the work fairly loose so that it can be 'pushed' into the correct position. Advanced applications for this technique are discussed in Chapters Two and Seven.

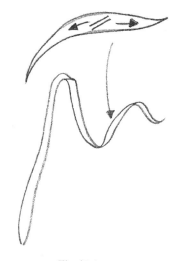

Fig A6 △
Snake stitch. One direction is always from the centre to the tip of a motif, the other from the centre to the core end

STRAIGHT STITCHING

Any technique which involves the use of either (1) single straight stitches to represent a whole motif, eg, a single blade of grass, or (2) straight stitches worked in unison, but without imitating *opus plumarium*; eg, horizontally to represent grassland, water, sky, etc, or in the perpendicular for tree trunks, etc.

SEED STITCHING

Worked directly on to the background fabric, not superimposed over other embroidery. Fine, very short straight stitches. Often used as the centres of flowers or leaves on distant trees (see centre of rose in Plate 74 and village scene in Plate 75).

CHEVRON STITCH

Used to convey any straight prickle or similar motif. Take two long straight stitches, angled to meet. Infill with a third straight stitch, if necessary. Using a finer thread, take a long straight stitch through the body of the spine, extending beyond the tip, if a particularly sharp tip is required.

'STRAIGHT' WINGS

Used for small insects in flight. Work a radial series of fine, straight stitches allowing the background fabric to show through. Never shadow line (see bee in Plate 74).

HONEYCOMB STITCH

Used for dragonfly's wings, etc. Transfer only the outline of the wing on to the fabric. Work fine radial stitches from the edge of the wing to the body of the insect. Lay a short stitch over two radial stitches at right angles and repeat, brickwork fashion. As these stitches are tightened the radial stitches will gradually be pulled in opposite directions to form a honeycomb pattern. Never shadow line. Overlay with specialist blending filament to create cellular sheen (see Fig A7).

DANDELION 'SHUTES'

May be used, adapted to shape and size, for any wind-blown seed. Using small straight stitches, worked close to the fabric, imitate the outline of the appropriate parachute. Added sheen may be achieved by the addition of seed stitches in fine metallic thread (see Plate 74).

COBWEBBING

Work a framework of outer threads. Add dissecting stitches similar to the spokes of a wheel. Whip around the spokes to suspend the body of the cobweb from the framework without stitching through the background fabric (see Fig A8).

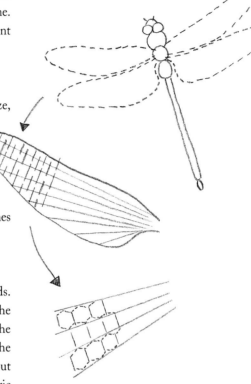

Fig A7 △

Honeycomb stitch. The 'brick' stitches must slightly overlap the radial stitches so that when they are tightened, they will gently separate the underlying work to reveal the honeycombing

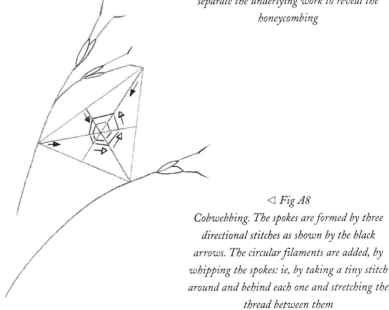

◁ Fig A8

Cobwebbing. The spokes are formed by three directional stitches as shown by the black arrows. The circular filaments are added, by whipping the spokes: ie, by taking a tiny stitch around and behind each one and stretching the thread between them

HELEN
STEVENS

SUBDUED VOIDING

Used to soften outlines where a less definite demarcation zone between fields is required, especially on animals and birds. Choose a colour which matches the upper plane, and, at exactly the same angle, work straight stitches in a fine thread spanning the voiding line (see squirrel in Plate 74).

NOTE: the next three techniques are best suited to matt fibres such as stranded cottons (eg, DMC) or twisted silks.

ETCHING

A method of shadowing used primarily on buildings in landscape work. Worked as a patch of perpendicular straight stitches (usually in black) below an overhanging feature (see village scene in Plate 75).

DOTTING

A technique mainly used for buildings. Very short, closely worked stitches arranged randomly and usually in a variety of colours, blending smoothly. Used to create grainy surfaces in close-up, or rough surfaces in the distance. Worked around etching (see village scene in Plate 75).

DASHING

Used to convey smooth surfaces in architectural embroidery, eg, plasterwork, thatches, etc. Worked in long, straight, perpendicular stitches from one field of etching, or other feature, to the next (see village scene in Plate 75).

FLOATING EMBROIDERY

A technique which allows threads to lie loosely on the background fabric, falling into spontaneous shapes. Do not transfer the design to be formed on to the background fabric. Take a long stitch from the inside to the outside of the motif, putting a finger under the thread to keep it away from the fabric. Take a very small stitch at the outer point to bring the thread back to the surface. Take a third stitch back to the core of the motif, again keeping a finger beneath the thread. Repeat the process, removing the finger when several strands have built up (see Fig A9).

MINIATURIZING

The process of extrapolating the essential features of a large study and translating them into miniature form. Usually, dalmatian dog technique is replaced by studding, and several strata of radial stitching reduced to a single field. The finest of threads are essential (see medallion in Plate 75).

◁ *PLATE 77*
Expanding the close-up techniques explored in Plate 76, together with landscape and other features, this sampler is inspired by work in The Embroiderer's Country Album *Embroidery shown life-size: 9 x 28.5cm (7½ x 11¼in)*

Fig A9 △
Small black arrows (1) indicate the outward stitch, a small stitch is taken at the apex, and open arrows (2) show the return of the thread to the core

THE PRACTICALITIES

WORKING CONDITIONS AND EQUIPMENT

LIGHTING

Daylight is the finest and most natural light of all but if daylight is not available or not sufficient a good spotlight is a worthwhile investment.

Always work with the spotlight in the same position in relation to your embroidery, so that you become familiar with the angle of the light. Any shadow cast by your hand will soon become unnoticeable. Keep the light in such a position that any shadow will not cut across the stitching.

If you are working on a fine fabric, avoid having a high level of light immediately behind the work, as this will have the effect of making the fabric transparent, and can be very distracting. If you are working outdoors keep the sun behind you, but wear a hat or use a sun shade, as concentration plus sunlight can lead to headaches and eyestrain.

EMBROIDERY FRAMES

In fine flat embroidery the tension of the background fabric is all important and it is essential to work on an embroidery frame. Round 'tambour' frames, so called because they resemble a tambourine, are best suited to fine work, as the tension they produce is entirely uniform. A free-standing frame is especially useful when techniques such as couching are to be included in the work, as these require two hands.

Tambour frames are available in a range of materials, but whichever frame is chosen it is essential that it should feel comfortable to use. If the diameter is more than approximately 35cm (14in) it can become too heavy, when dressed, to be hand-held without making the arm tired, so it should therefore be free-standing. Ideally, a hand-held tambour frame should be small enough for the fingers of the hand in which it is held to reach from the outer rim to the centre of the frame without straining, as they will be able to guide the needle when it is on the reverse of the fabric. For free-standing frames, a good rule of thumb is that the embroiderer should be able to reach to the centre of the dressed frame without stretching unduly when the elbow is at the level of the outer rim.

OTHER EQUIPMENT

The choice of smaller tools is a personal one. Embroidery scissors must be small, fine and sharp, whatever their design. The finer your choice of threads, the sharper and keener the scissors must be.

Needles, too, must be chosen with the specific use of threads and fabric in mind. It is a good idea to have a selection of various sizes to avoid frustration when a new piece of work is begun. Sizes 5 to 10 are generally the most useful. For metallic threads use either a wide-eyed embroidery needle or a crewel needle of suitable size, depending on the technique.

If you use a thimble, be sure that it fits snugly and be careful that it has no worn or jagged edged which may catch in the work – this applies to all the tools discussed.

Fig B1 △
With the thumb on the outer ring of the tambour frame, the fingers of the hand should just be able to reach the centre of the circle. Similarly, with a larger frame, with the elbow at the ring, the fingers should reach the centre

MATERIALS

There are no 'right' or 'wrong' choices when it comes to choosing fabric and thread so long as certain practical considerations are borne in mind. For so-called flat-work embroidery which must be worked in a frame, it is essential that the fabric chosen for the background does not stretch. If it stretches even slightly while embroidery is in progress, when removed from the frame it will contract to its normal size, and the embroidery will be distorted.

Larger pictures should be worked on heavier fabrics, smaller studies on light-weights, but this rule can be adapted to the particular needs of the picture in question.

Try to avoid fabrics with too loose a weave, as too many stitches will be vying for space in too few threads of warp and weft and the result will be unsatisfactory. Pure cotton and linen evenweaves are ideal, but as a general rule for this type of 'freestyle' embroidery, if the weave is open enough to be used for counted thread embroidery it is too wide for us!

The choice of threads depends upon a number of factors. *Stranded cottons*, such as DMC, are adaptable and widely available in a large range of colours. When split down into single threads they can be delicate enough to convey all but the finest details, and are fine enough to allow themselves to be 'mixed' in the needle. Avoid those skeins which vary their shades throughout their length; they are rarely convincing. It is better to re-thread your needle several times with slightly different shades. Shiny rayons and nylons can also be attractive, but their colours may not be as natural as you could wish, so choose carefully.

Pure silk threads are, of course, the finest and most enjoyable to use, though their behaviour in the needle can be frustrating to beginners. There are many different types of silk thread to choose from. 'Floss' silks are untwisted and therefore very shiny. The advantage of using floss is that it can be split down into very fine threads for the minutest detailed work, and then used doubled, or even trebled, to describe the more substantial parts of the design. For this reason it is ideal when it comes to 'mixing' colours in the needle. An almost infinite variety of shades can be achieved, which is particularly important for natural history subjects. The disadvantage of floss is that by virtue of its untwisted state it can fragment in the needle during the course of working, and, especially if you have rough skin, can catch, fray and generally become very irritating! One solution to this problem is to make sure that your hands remain as smooth and soft as possible, and remember that a rough fingernail (or any other jagged edge) can damage your work almost beyond repair if it catches in embroidery already in situ.

Twisted silks are slightly easier to work with and also have a glorious shine. If they are not twisted too tightly, they may be split down into finer strands for detailed work, and then used in their original state for covering large areas. They are also useful in combination with floss silks to describe areas which do not require such a high level of sheen, for instance, buildings, roads and other man-made aspects of country life.

Stranded silks are a fairly recent innovation. These are a great boon to anyone used to stranded cottons, as they are in similar format and may be used either split into single threads or as up

Note: Much of the information contained in Appendix B is explained in greater detail in *The Embroiderer's Countryside*, pages 125–34 and *The Embroiderer's Country Album*, pages 129–41.

Fig B2 ▷
Loop the strands loosely over the right hand, palm facing you. Drop them over the hook, and pull taut

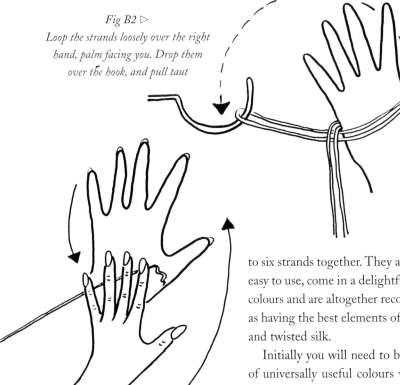

Fig B3 △
Holding the strand(s) firmly against the heel of the right hand, roll them upwards with the fingertips of the left. Bringing the left hand downwards at the same rate helps to create a smoother thread

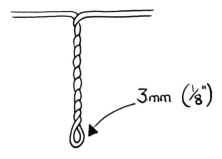

3mm (⅛")

Fig B4 △
Scale x 2 approximately. Releasing the tension allows the thread to twist on to itself. If the correct tension has been achieved it should do so smoothly, form the appropriate loop and disentangle itself easily when pulled straight

to six strands together. They are flexible, easy to use, come in a delightful range of colours and are altogether recommended as having the best elements of both floss and twisted silk.

Initially you will need to buy a range of universally useful colours which will adapt themselves to your preferred subject matter. Decide upon about six basics and get up to three shades of each. For instance, green is obviously a prerequisite of any countryside embroidery project, so buy a true mid-toned green, together with a paler version of the same colour and a darker one for shadowing, etc. Similarly with browns, pinks, blues, yellow-orange and lilac. Needless to say, white and black are also essentials.

The choice of *metallic thread* is wide and varied; plan an excursion to a good needlework shop and have fun choosing for yourself!

Finally, of course, there are all the little extras which make collecting threads and materials more than a practical job and take it into the realms of fantasy. Specialist threads, tiny seed pearls and beads, and the occasional sequin and feather all deserve a place in some secret little glory-hole at the back of your workbox.

TWISTING FLOSS SILK

As you become more advanced in your designs you may find that you wish to mix several types of thread in a single picture – for instance a pure silk embroidery may need to incorporate a number of different textures in the same colours. Silk is expensive but it is possible to effectively double your range of colours by learning the simple technique of plying or twisting, thus creating a finished silk thread with a matt lustre rather than a high gloss.

When using several strands of silk together in the needle to create a single thread (such as when mixing colours), the single thread created is referred to as being *two into one* (written 2/1) or *three into one* (3/1) and so on depending upon how many strands are being used. This may be followed by 'F' or 'T' to denote either free or twisted. The most easily created twists are 2/1T and 4/1T. When practising the technique it is best to use fairly thick strands; finer gauges can be used later. You will need something around which to loop your thread as you twist (see Figs B2, B3, and B4). If possible, find a spot where you can screw in a cup-hook and leave it for future use. Whatever you use it must be unmoving and thin. To create a 2/1T:

1 Cut a length of floss about 90cm (3ft) long.

2 Catch it around the hook and even up the ends. Holding both ends in your left hand, create a loop with your right hand and drop the loop over the hook. Move one strand around the hook so that a single strand is coming from each side.

3 Take the strand coming from the right of the hook and hold it against the

heel of the right hand with the fingertips of the left. Roll the strand up the right hand, catch it at the fingertips and repeat.

4 Release the tension on about a third of the strand. The loop formed should be about 3mm (⅛in) across.

5 Pull the twisted strand to one side and tape it to a firm object to prevent it from unwinding. Repeat steps 3 and 4 above with the other strand, twisting it in the same direction. You have now *undertwisted* your thread.

6 Bringing the two twisted strands together, make the first motion of a simple knot, by passing one end over the other. Hold the ends of both strands against the heel of the left hand with the right fingertips and roll the strands up the left hand. Check the tension by repeating step 4 above, but this time the reverse twist should mean that the thread will not form a loop. If the ply is too loose (ie, the thread is not holding together) apply a further reverse twist. The thread is now *overtwisted* and ready to use.

To create a 4/1T, the same procedure is followed, substituting a pair of strands on either side of the hook for the single strand used in a 2/1T.

For a 3/1T it is necessary to split one of the single strands in half in order that you can twist one and a half strands on either side of the hook.

USING BLENDING FILAMENTS

Blending filaments (fine specialist threads containing cellophane or metallic strands) are intended to be used in conjunction with other threads to highlight and emphasize features. They can either be used loosely in a 2/1F thread, making up half the thickness of the thread, more subtly as a smaller percentage of a 3/1F or 4/1F, or twisted into a 2/1T, 3/1T or 4/1T, making a much more compact thread. To use them in twisted threads, follow the procedures set out above, substituting the blending filament for as many strands of the finished thread as you require.

They may also be split down into their essential elements, giving the opportunity of including a fine cellophane strand alone with floss silk, or twisted into a very narrow 2/1T.

TRANSLATING YOUR SKETCHES

Whether you are working from your own sketch, from a design suggested by the drawings in this book, or from a photograph or pre-prepared design, the first step is to transfer the pattern from paper to fabric. It is important to remember that every line which is transferred on to your background fabric is there permanently, and must therefore be covered by embroidery. Very fine details should be omitted from the

Fig B5 ▽
When planning your design, you may like to use the classical 'perfect dimension' of 16:9, on which the Parthenon was based. Seen empty, the resulting rectangle seems elongated, but the dimension becomes easily filled and is strangely harmonious to the human eye. It can be used landscape or portrait

transfer process, as fine embroidery would not be heavy enough to disguise the transferred line. Such fine detail must be worked freehand at a later date.

For transferring a design to fabric you will need:

- Tracing paper
- A large piece of firm cardboard (or wooden drawing board)
- Straight pins (drawing pins)
- Dull pencil, or other stylus
- Ruler
- Dressmaker's carbon paper (dressmaker's tracing paper)
- A flat, smooth table
- Background fabric (remember to leave a large border around your work for mounting)

Tracing paper is available in various weights. A good weight is approximately 90gsm, but you may need to undertake a little trial and error before you find the right weight for your chosen fabric.

DO NOT be tempted to use a typewriter carbon paper. The carbon

will rub off on the fabric and is very difficult to remove. Dressmaker's carbon paper (or dressmaker's tracing paper) which is available in most fabric and embroidery stores and haberdashery departments is designed specifically for our purposes. It can usually be bought in packets of assorted colours and has a hard, waxy finish.

METHOD

1 Make a tracing of the chosen design. Place a sheet of tracing paper (this may have to be cut to size) over the pattern and carefully draw over each line with a lead pencil. In any large areas of the design which will be entirely covered by embroidery, you may wish to indicate the direction of stitching by shading. Check that you have traced all the required information (minus fine detail) before removing the paper from the design.

2 Place the cardboard on a flat surface, and lay your fabric out on it. If you use a wooden drawing board make sure that it is padded with several sheets of lining paper as this is necessary to produce a smooth, even line. Carefully position the traced design over the fabric, making sure that the 'north/south' alignment of the design is in line with the weave of the fabric. If the design is to be centred, use a ruler to find the midpoint. Pin the design to the fabric and into the board at the four corners, using the drawing pins.

Do not forget the importance of leaving a good sized border around your work, for effect as well as mounting. Your design may suddenly look very small on a large expanse of fabric, but this is only an illusion.

Fig B6 ▽
The carbon paper, shown partly hatched, is interleaved carefully between the background fabric and the design paper

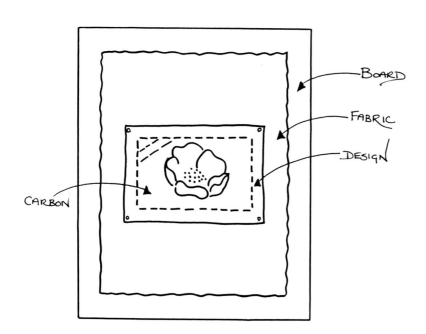

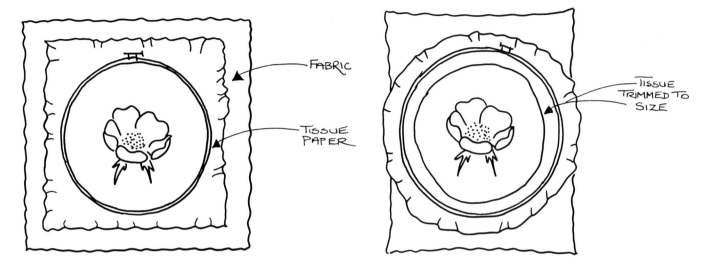

3 Choose a sheet of carbon paper in a colour which contrasts to your fabric. (White 'chalked' carbon paper will rub off as work progresses, so beginners may prefer to use the more waxy yellow or orange carbon paper on dark fabrics.)

Slip the carbon, colour side down, between the tracing and the fabric, removing one of the corner pins to do so. Replace the pin. Do not pin through the carbon paper. Using your pencil (your pencil should be dull, as a sharp pencil applying a hard pressure to the tracing paper will damage it) trace a few lines of the design. Remove one of the pins, raise one corner of the tracing and the carbon and check the impression. If the result is too heavy, apply slightly less pressure, if it is too light, a little more pressure. Replace the sheets and the pin and trace the whole of the design through on to the fabric. Take care not to smudge the carbon by resting your hand on top of the tracing while working, and do not let the pencil mark the fabric.

4 Remove the carbon and all but two of the top pins and check that all the design is transferred before removing the tracing.

PREPARING THE EMBROIDERY

There are various methods of 'dressing' a tambour frame and you should chose that one that suits you best. The procedure set out below has the advantage of not adding any weight to a hand-held frame and it may be used on all types and sizes of tambour frames.

1 Lay the inner ring of the tambour on a flat, clean surface.

2 Over this, place a sheet of tissue paper. If a large frame is used (ie larger than the individual sheets of paper) cut the tissue into wide strips and stick them loosely to the ring using double-sided sticky tape.

3 Position the fabric over this, and put a second sheet of tissue paper over both. If a large frame is used, cut wide strips of the paper and lay them around the edges of the work.

4 Position the outer ring of the frame over the whole ensemble and press down smoothly but firmly. If using a keyed frame, tighten the screw to the appropriate tension.

Fig B7 (above left) △
The tissue paper lies on top of the fabric, the upper ring of the frame ready to hold the two together. The design would be hidden beneath the tissue at this stage; it is shown here to indicate its position within the frame

Fig B8 (above right) △
Once mated with its lower counterparts, the frame becomes whole, sandwiching two layers of tissue and fabric. The tissue is then cut away top and bottom to reveal the design, and conveniently trimmed around the outside of the ring for ease of handling

5 Cut away the tissue paper to reveal the design beneath. Turn the frame over and cut away the tissue paper at the back to reveal the underside of the work. The remaining paper will protect the edges and avoid leaving a 'ring' around your finished work.

WORKING LARGE CANVASES

From time to time you may wish to work an embroidery which is too large to fit even a free-standing quilter's tambour frame. Special procedures must be followed in these cases, and great care taken that in moving the embroidery within the frame no damage is caused to the embroidery already completed, and no smudges created in the transferred design. Using a large cartoon as an example (Fig B9), it is clear that only approximately half the design will comfortably fit the frame at any one time.

1 Decide which section of the embroidery you wish to work first. (If you are right handed this will be the left-hand section and vice versa if you are left handed.) Cover the inner ring of the frame with tissue paper as described above and lay the appropriate section of the fabric in position.

2 Place a second sheet of tissue paper over the fabric (as above) but where the transferred design is to be held between the rings of the frame place an extra couple of sheets as added padding.

3 Position the outer ring with the key (if any) at the top, press down and tighten as before.

4 Cut away the excess tissue paper to reveal the section to be worked (similarly on the reverse).

Fig B9 ▽
The work, 62 x 26cm (24½ x 10in), is to be mounted on a backing board of 72 x 36cm (28½ x 14in), indicated by the outer line. Enough fabric must also be allowed for folding under and turning back (see Figs B13 and B14). Worked on a free-standing tambour frame 56cm (22in) across, it is important that the 'cut off' line (shown broken) should pass through an area containing as little activity as possible, allowing the two areas to be worked independently and merged as smoothly as possible

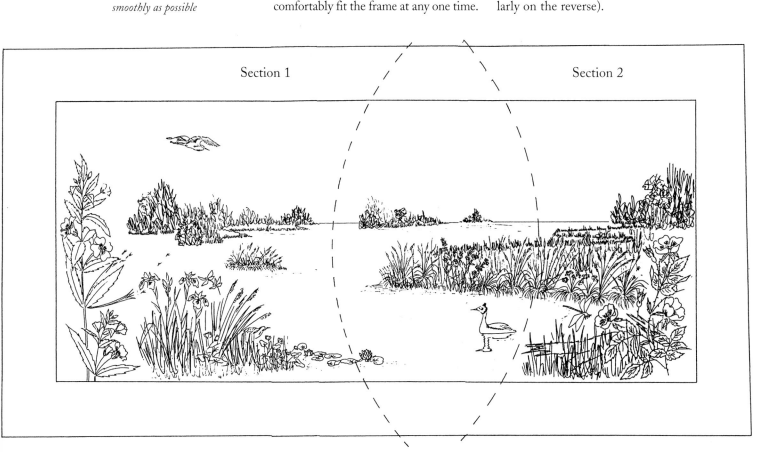

Section 1   Section 2

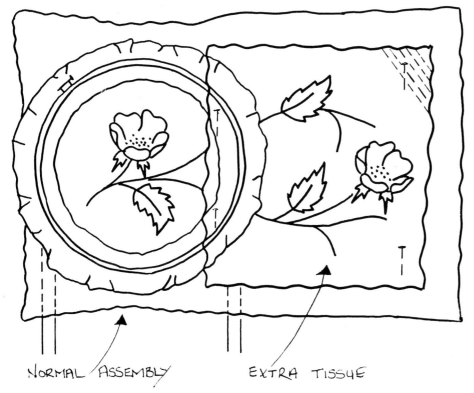

NORMAL ASSEMBLY   EXTRA TISSUE

◁ *Fig B10*
If possible, lay even a free-standing frame flat to achieve this assembly. The additional tissue paper, shown partly hatched, is pinned loosely over the section of the design to be protected

5 Pin a large sheet of tissue paper to the fabric, extending sideways to protect the design still outside the frame. Roll up the fabric with the tissue paper inside to protect the transfer and tape it to the edge of the frame.

6 When the first section of the embroidery has been completed, dismantle the frame and repeat the procedure above. Take particular care when assembling the rings positioned over embroidery already worked, and at step 5 use several sheets of tissue paper to pad out and protect the fabric to be rolled up as this time it will include the embroidery itself!

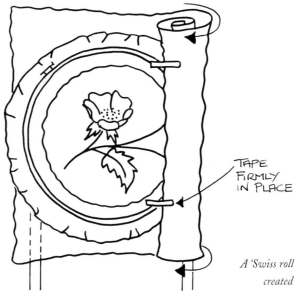

TAPE FIRMLY IN PLACE

◁ *Fig B11*
A 'Swiss roll' of fabric and tissue paper is created and taped to the frame

WORKING A PAIR OF EMBROIDERIES
It is possible to economize on fabric, while still enjoying the flexibility of a free-standing frame, by working a pair of small embroideries at the same time on one frame. During the transfer process position the designs as shown in Fig B12. If you are left handed they will be mirrored. Make sure that you leave enough room between the two for them to be separated when work is complete and remember this must allow for the

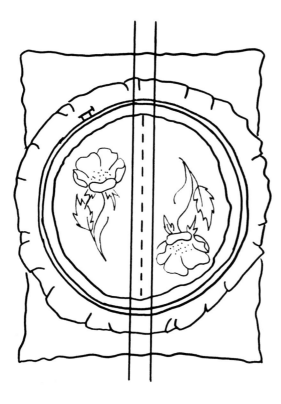

Fig B12 △

If two embroideries are to be worked on a single frame, remember to allow enough fabric between the pair for mounting

- Acid-free cartridge paper cut to the same size, white for work on a pale ground, black for work on black
- Clear sticky tape
- Fabric scissors
- Two large-eyed needles
- Lacing thread (mercerized cotton, or similar thread which will not stretch)
- Iron and ironing board

METHOD

1 Press the embroidery on the wrong side, without steam (after checking the manufacturer's instructions for fabric and thread).

2 Using a small amount of sticky tape, secure the cartridge paper to the surface of the board.

3 Position the embroidery right side up over the covered board, and leaving a margin of at least 4cm (1½in) cut the fabric to size. Leave a larger margin for larger pieces of work or for heavy fabric.

4 Carefully, and without shifting the position of the embroidery in relation to the board, turn the whole ensemble over so that the embroidery is face down, with the board on top of it. Make sure you are working on a clean surface.

5 Cut a long but manageable piece of lacing thread, and thread a needle at each end of the thread, with two 'tails' of similar length.

6 Fold the two sides of the fabric to the centre of the board.

7 Working from the top, insert a needle on either side and lace the two sides of the fabric together corset

border around the work necessary for mounting etc. Position the key (if any) away from either of the designs.

At all times when not in use your frame and its precious contents should be covered and kept clean. Work on pale fabric, in particular, is vulnerable to the least speck of dirt. Always wash your hands before beginning to embroider and throw a cover over your frame if you leave it unattended – particularly if you are working outdoors!

PRESENTATION

MOUNTING

For mounting, you will need:
- Hardboard (or very stiff cardboard) cut to the size of the finished work (remember to make this big enough for the framing, and smooth off the edges thoroughly)

fashion until you reach the bottom. If you run out of lacing thread, simply tie the thread off and begin again with more thread.

8 Fold the top and bottom of the fabric towards the centre and repeat the lacing process. It takes a little practice to achieve perfect tension. Do not over-tighten the laces as they may break, or rip the fabric, but do not be afraid of creating a reasonable pull on the work as only in this way will the original tension of the

fabric on the tambour be re-created. Always tie off the ends of the lacing thread with firm, non-slip knots, and snip off any extra thread which is left.

MOUNTING LARGE EMBROIDERIES
Particular care must be taken when preparing a large embroidery for mounting. The larger the canvas, the greater the tension which may be needed to keep it taut on its backing board. Before lacing, therefore, the edges of the work should be turned

◁ *Fig B13*
Mounting the embroidery:
a Embroidery is placed face down, backing board positioned on top
b The outer sides of the fabric are folded in
c They are laced, corset fashion
d The top and bottom edges of the fabric are treated similarly

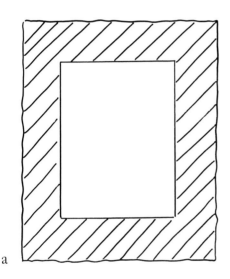

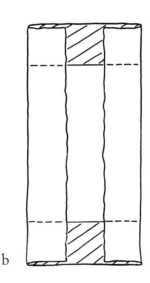

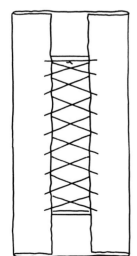

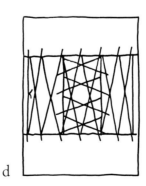

a

b

c

d

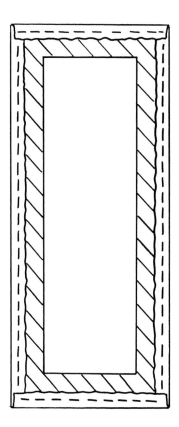

Fig B14 ▷
With the embroidery face down and the board
in position, turn back a 'hem' of fabric and tack
in position. When lacing the work in place
stitch through both layers of the hem for added
strength when mounting a large or oddly
proportioned piece

back to allow the lacing thread to pass through two thicknesses of fabric. When put under pressure the fabric will be less likely to tear.

When mounting a long, narrow embroidery (such as that featured in Fig B9) lace whichever dimension is the greater first. Do not pull the lacing too tight, as even a rigid backing board, such as hardboard, will bow if put under excessive tension.

CIRCULAR OR OVAL MOUNTS
Repeat steps 1 to 4 under 'Method' on page 138, but leave a slightly larger border of fabric around the backing board.

5 Cut a piece of lacing thread the length of the circumference of the circle of fabric and thread a single large-eyed needle.

6 Work a line of running stitch approximately 3 or 4cm (1–1½in) inside the edge of the fabric, leaving the ends of the lacing thread on the right side of the embroidery.

7 Check that the design is still centrally located and draw up the running stitches. Tie off the thread and snip off the excess.

8 The pleats of fabric which have been formed by drawing up the lacing thread will be standing proud. Using an iron at the correct temperature press them firmly all in one direction.

MINIATURES
The basic process for mounting miniatures is similar to that described above for either straight-edged, circular or oval work. However, remember that your frame will be a great deal smaller, not only in width and height, but also in depth (ie, rebate; see 'Framing' below). The margin of fabric to be turned back, while wide enough to safely accept the lacing thread, should be as narrow as possible to avoid bulk; similarly the lacing thread itself. It should not be necessary to exert great tension on a very small piece, as the embroidery itself will be very light.

It is particularly important to check that there are no specks of dust, fluff or tiny pieces of silk adhering to the front of a miniature before framing. Something the size of a pinhead, which might be overlooked on a larger piece, will assume major proportions on a study only two inches high. It is a good idea always to make a careful inspection of the front of the work, whatever its size, before moving on to the final stage or presentation.

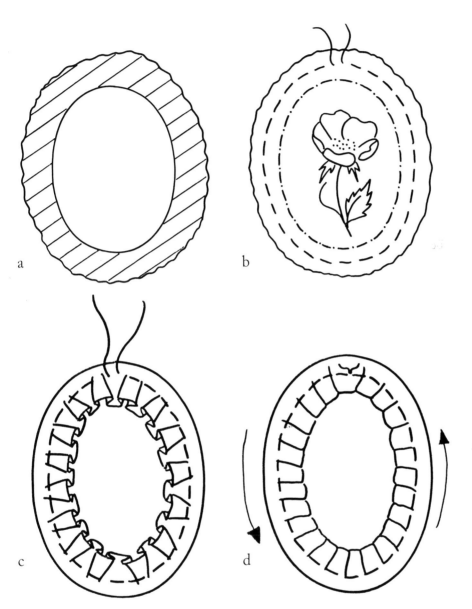

◁ Fig B15
a Embroidery face down, the oval mounting board is placed on top
b Face up (position of mounting board indicated by dot/dash line) running stitches are worked around the edge of the fabric
c Draw up the running stitches to form a series of pleats
d Press all the pleats in one direction to reduce bulk

FRAMING

The choice of frame is a personal matter, but always be prepared to take professional advice, as framing can make or mar a picture. On a practical level, the rebate on any frame must be deep enough to accommodate the mounted work, the window mount required to lift the glass from the work (essential if beads etc have been used), the glass and a sheet of cardboard holding the ensemble together.

Avoid hanging work immediately above radiators or fireplaces, and avoid bathrooms and kitchens. No picture should be hung in direct prolonged sunlight. However, to be seen to their best advantage, embroideries need a good level of lighting and ordinary daylight will do little harm. A small spotlight positioned so that it illuminates the work from above will bring it to life, especially in the evenings. Take a little time to achieve the most effective angle of lighting.

SELECT BIBLIOGRAPHY

Anon, Beowulf from *Anglo-Saxon Poetry* (translated by R. K. Gordon, Everyman Library no 1794)

Anon, *Pangur Ban*, eighth-century manuscript (translated by Robin Flower, Pelham Books Ltd, London 1984)

Anon, *Sir Gawain and the Green Knight* (translated by J. R. R. Tolkein, George Allen and Unwin, 1975)

Anon, *The Mabinogion* (translated by Gwyn Jones and Thomas Jones, Everyman Library, 1949)

Bevis, Trevor, *Fenland Saints and Sanctuaries* (Cambridge, 1997)

Fitzgerald, Edward, *The Rubaiyat of Omar Khayyam* (1859) (The Richards Press, London, 1940)

Gerard, John, *Gerard's Herbal, The History of Plants* (Senate Studio Editions Ltd, 1994)

Kipling, Rudyard, *The Just So Stories* (Macmillan and Co, London, 1903)

Shakespeare, William, *The Complete Works* (Nelson Doubleday Inc, New York, 1968)

Stevens, Helen M., *The Embroiderer's Country Album* (David & Charles, 1994)
      The Embroiderer's Countryside (David & Charles, 1992)
      The Timeless Art of Embroidery (David & Charles, 1997)

Stewart, Bob, *Where is St George? Pagan Imagery in English Folksong* (Moonraker Press, 1977)

Various authors, *Fairies, An Anthology of Verse and Prose* (Arness Publishing, 1996)

Various authors, *The School Book of English Verse* (Macmillan and Co, 1938)

Howson, John, *Songs Sung in Suffolk* (Veteran Tapes)

ACKNOWLEDGEMENTS

In addition to my thanks to those inhabitants of the Perilous Realm who aided in the preparation of this book, I am also grateful to the professionals – Nigel Salmon, photographer; Cheryl Brown and everyone at David & Charles – and to all those who so generously passed on their knowledge of mythology, fairy tales, folk songs and lore. Without the oral tradition of story-telling this book could not have come about. Thanks, too, to my family (who have weathered the crisis of yet another deadline!) and to Ragnar Hairybritches.

Clients who generously allowed their pictures to be included in this book are: Mrs Sheila Wakerley (Plates 1, 60.1 and 60.2); Irene Izzard (Plate 6); Miss Zara Plumb (Plate 7); Mrs Gail Bulman (Plate 8); Mrs Sharon Greenwood (Plates 13 and 27); Pam and Frank Bacon (Plate 14); Mrs Janice Huntingford (Plate 16); Val Lynas (Plate 31); Mrs Margaret Bailey (Plate 33); Mrs Pat Wood (Plate 37); Maris Stibbon (Plate 41); Master James Plumb (Plate 46); Av Steele (Plate 59); Pam Brownsea (Plate 74).

Embroideries in Plates 42 and 65 first appeared in *Needlework Magazine*, and Plate 26 in *Needlecraft Magazine*, published by Future Publishing.

INDEX